ISSUES AND CHALLENGES OF CONVERTIBILITY

ISSUES AND CHALLENGES OF CONVERTIBILITY

G. PANNERSELVAM

ABHIJEET PUBLICATIONS
DELHI 110094

ABHIJEET PUBLICATIONS
2/46 Tukhmeerpur Extension
Delhi-110 094
Phone: 011-22960492, 65698474
E-mail: abhijeetpublication@gmail.com

ISSUES AND CHALLENGES OF CONVERTIBILITY

First Published 2008

ISBN 978-81-89886-96-7

PRINTED IN INDIA

Published by J.K. Singh for Abhijeet Publications, Delhi-110 094, Lasertypeset by Gaurav Graphics, New Delhi and Printed at Himanshu Printers, Delhi.

than it is for an emerging market, in which growth has to be largely export-led. I am not arguing that emerging markets benefit themselves by running undervalued exchange rates and continuous export surpluses; real resources are best used for real investment at home, not for buying lots of US treasury bills. But it is a mistake, especially critical for an emerging market, to allow its exchange rate to be pushed up to an uncompetitive level. This consideration suggests that current Indian exchange rate policy is sensibly balanced, whereas any rapid move to liberalise capital flows could create problems for maintaining that balance.

The conditions suggested by the first Tarapore Committee omitted one important consideration. Specifically, the committee did not acknowledge the fundamental importance of having become completely trusted in international markets. When a mature industrial country gets into trouble and wishes to borrow more in order to tide over bad times, it can always do so, because lenders do not doubt that it will be able and willing to continue servicing its debts. Markets may charge more, or exchange rates may depreciate, but ultimately industrial countries can continue to borrow if they need to and are willing to pay the price. Unfortunately this is not true for emerging markets, even if they have an exemplary past record of debt service. And the fact that some of them don't (think of Argentina as the most recent example) does not make it easier for the others. Situations in which markets simply will not lend, on any terms, have continued to recur in recent years, until the cyclical upswing started in 2003 and avoided further crises for the moment. Think of Latin American countries, like Brazil in 2002 or Chile in 1998. Or think of the Asian crisis (a particularly vivid example). Or, to go slightly further back in history, think of India itself in 1991.

This is not to argue that India and other emerging markets never should or will have capital account convertibility. As they grow and as per capita income increases it is to be expected both that market thus will increase and the efficacy of capita controls will fall. If a country becomes; net creditor to the rest of the world, it can expect greater returns if it out of the economic literature on capital account liberalisation, and all three are completely reasonable. In addition, the literature suggests that countries need to have liberalised their trade regime before accepting large capital inflows, so that one could expect the profitability of in vestment to be closely correlated with the social returns to the investment, rather than having investment flow into profitable but socially inefficient import-substituting industries.

Progress in Two Areas

In the nine years since it last considered capital account liberalisation, India has made important progress in two of the three areas specified by the first Tarapore Committee as preconditions, and in liberalising trade. Inflation has fallen from over 7 per cent in 1997 to under 4 per cent in 2005, and the RBI has been told to pursue an inflation target. The percentage of advances classified as non-performing—which is the best single measure of the health of the banking system—has fallen from 13.7 per cent in March 1997 to 5.2 per cent in March 2005. And while Indian trade is still far from completely free, it is now far less restricted than it then was: in particular, the quotas on imports of consumer goods have now been phased out. Unfortunately that still leaves one important area in which India has not made progress, which concerns fiscal discipline: the total size of the public sector deficit has actually risen from 7.3 per cent of GDP in 1997-98 to an estimated 7.7 per cent of GDP in 2005-06 (with even higher figures in between), while the ratio of public debt to GDP has increased from under 65 per cent to over 83 per cent. So even on the conditions suggested by the first Tarapore Committee, a quick move to capital account convertibility would be premature.

It is worth noting also that the first Tarapore Committee rightly argued that acceptance of capital account convertibility presupposed a pretty flexible exchange rate policy, so that a change in capital flows could be absorbed by a change in the exchange rate rather than a surfeit of reserves or their possible exhaustion. But this in turn is something that is easier for an advanced industrial country to fully accept

Contents

more important, because of the desire for cheaper credit on the part of Indian business, which looked with envy at the relatively low dollar interest rates prevailing in the outside world and contrasted them with the high rupee interest rates then prevalent in India. Indian business wanted to be able to access cheap external credit without having to ask permission of the Reserve Bank of India.

The desire was understandable, but the cost of giving in to it would have been to expose India to the danger of contagion similar to that which laid the whole of east Asia low when Thailand had a balance of payments problem. For there is no serious doubt that the countries that suffered crises in 1997 were those that had accepted a large volume of short-term capital and not those that were particularly corrupt. Like China, India was not among them, not because there is no corruption in China or India, but because they did not have an open capital account and therefore had not imported a lot of capital that could flee when investors panicked.

Tarapore Conditions

Should India now change its policy and allow free flows of capital, including short-term loans, by all and sundry? The first Tarapore Committee specified three preconditions that needed to be satisfied before it would be sensible to move to capital account convertibility. First, the country needed to have established fiscal discipline to make sure that capital inflows did not provide an easy way of perpetuating what is ultimately unsustainable. A failure to do this would eventually lead to a crisis when the market finally decided to cease financing the deficit. Second, the country needed to reduce the rate of inflation to the range of 3 to 5 per cent per year, and to make the pursuit of an inflation target the central mandate of the Reserve Bank of India. Third, India needed to have cleaned up its banking system, so that one could be confident that capital inflows would be efficiently intermediated to where they would be profitably invested, rather than used by banks to borrow more with the object of postponing bankruptcy. These conditions come squarely evidence to support the conjecture that a complete absence of controls brings faster growth or other economic benefits What this surely suggests is that what is usually the last step in liberalising the capital account, namely, the liberalisation of short-term loans, may bring costs that outweigh the benefits. It is not difficult to believe this. All the evidence is that bank flows—which are the part of the capital account that is separately recorded and that falls most clearly in the short-term loan category—are highly volatile. As soon as a developing country hits a difficult patch, whether because of low prices of the commodities it exports or political uncertainties or contagion from neighbours, bank loans are liquidated—and (unlike equity investments, where the investor at least tends to pay through the nose for surrendering to panic) they can be liquidated without cost to the lender.

Risk of Short-Term Loans

The charge of critics is that short-term loans contribute nothing to welfare. They cannot safely be used to expand investment, since they may be withdrawn before the investment project matures. They tend to disappear just when they could play a useful role in helping to smooth consumption. (Remember the old adage that a banker only lends to those who do not need the money.) And inherently they do not provide an instrument for portfolio diversification. Yet it is primarily variations in the flow of short-term capital, like bank loans, that give rise to the pro-cyclicality of the capital account, which provides the main mechanism by which free capital flows create problems. (Some people would add tax evasion as another channel for creating problems, but I do not discuss that consideration in this article.)

Why, then, was there so much pressure in India for liberalisation of the capital account in 1997, when the first Tarapore Committee (1997) proposed "gradual" (over three years!) liberalisation of the capital account? For two main reasons. First, because that was the spirit of the age, (before the Asian crisis), as manifest in the pressures on the IMF recalled at the beginning of this article. Second, and doubtless the partner country should commit itself to never reimposing effective capital controls for any length of time. Several of the partner countries that had made effective use of such controls in the past, like Chile and Singapore, found themselves forced to choose between abandoning their aim of securing a free trade agreement with the US and abandoning their ability to control capital movements with the object of avoiding or at least attenuating crises. Given that governments, like markets, typically take a rather short-term view of costs and benefits, and that the countries could not see the prospect of a crisis on the horizon at the time the negotiations were taking place, the US treasury got its way.

But elsewhere the pressure to move to capital account liberalisation seemed to have disappeared. In particular, IMF research—which one may assume was inclined to find support for capital account liberalisation if a serious case could be made—concluded that there is at best mixed evidence of net benefits from free capital flows [Prasad et al 2003].

Note that this does not argue that there are no benefits from certain types of capital flow. There is overwhelming reason (and abundant empirical evidence) to think that foreign direct investment is highly beneficial, because it provides an efficient mechanism for spreading the fruits of technological innovation and intellectual property around the world. There is also solid empirical evidence to believe that liberalising the flow of portfolio investment is beneficial, because it reduces the cost of capital to enterprises and it enables investors to gain the benefits of diversification [Henry 2000a, b]. Hence it is not at all surprising that in some empirical studies [such as Quinn 1997], where the question asked is whether liberalisation of the capital account is beneficial, a positive result should have been obtained, since many of the liberalising moves that provide the independent variable in such studies referred to liberalisation of FDI or portfolio investment.

But the studies in Prasad et al (2003) are not of this type. They ask whether countries without capital controls do better than countries with them, and they failed to find

1

Convertibility and Its Genesis

During the 1990s there was a rather widespread belief that free international capital movements were as much a part of a liberal economy as free product markets, a liberalised domestic financial system, or free trade. So strongly was this belief held that in 1997 the IMF was on the verge of extending its remit to include supervision of controls on international capital flows, with an objective of helping its member countries to move progressively to a situation where they had no such controls. The IMF's Interim Committee (now renamed the International Monetary and Financial Committee) affirmed its intention of having the IMF amend its articles to that effect during the annual meeting in Hong Kong in September 1997, after the Asian crisis had already swept through south-east Asia but before it had engulfed Hong Kong and Korea. Considered reflection on the causes of that crisis subsequently led to abandonment of the project to extend the Fund's remit to cover capital flows, with its presumption that freeing capital movements was a priority on the reform agenda.

Since then the main pressure for liberalising capital flows has come from the US treasury. When countries wanted to negotiate bilateral free trade agreements with the US, they found the treasury insisted that US negotiators demand that

I feel happy to thank my Father-in-Law, Mother-in-Law, Brother, Sister and Daughter without their constant pressure and co-operation.

I am thankful to Abhijeet Publications New Delhi for their Interest and co-operation in publishing this book.

I do not claim that could cover all the aspects of the convertibility within the limited space, but I firmly believe that this book will be very useful to all concerned.

G. PANNEERSELVAM

Thanjavur

July 2008

Preface

Convertibility is the best tool in the hands of monetary authority of a country to adjust monetary disequilibrium. Monetary disequilibrium arises due to heavy down payment of one country's currency. In the international arena, one country's currency is adjusted interms of another country's currency, so as to make international trade in a larger quantity. Many financial crises have been settled with the help of convertibility.

Most industrialized economics like Brazil, Mexico and other Latin American countries experienced with the Full convertibility Technique. India is also trying to follow full convertibility but the results are only lesser than the expectation. This book made an attempt to bring out all the possible avenues of monetary equilibrium.

To thank profusely scholars and authorities is a pleasure indeed.

I am greatly indebted to Dr. A. Arunachalam, M.A., M. Phil., M.L., Ph.D., M.B.A., Chairman and Correspondent of Adaikalamatha College, Vallam, Thanjavur.

I owe my sincere thanks to respected Principal Dr. R. KATHIAN, M.Com., M.Phil., Ph.D., for his timely help.

Dedicated To

My Beloved Parents

M. GOVINDHASAMY

&

NAGAMMAL

allows most of its investments to be made by private the authorities in US treasury bills or similar low-yielding instruments they like to hold (so as to avoid the charge of losing public money, which they do not expect to be levelled against them as long as the securities do not depreciate in terms of the US dollar). A time will therefore come when it will be entirely appropriate for the state to allow free capital flows. Judging by the European experience after the Second World War, it takes about 30 years from when a country starts the process of liberalisation and financial integration before it makes sense to move to capital account convertibility. That is why I told an Indian newspaper in 1997 that I thought the first Tarapore report's proposals were about 30 years premature. Maybe I suggested five or 10 years more than is necessary, but I still don't think I overestimated by 21 years. Of course, countries do not suffer capital flight when their central banks are sitting on reserves of $ 140 billion odd (approaching 20 per cent of GDP) and a world boom is in progress. But the case for restraint in moving to capital account convertibility does not rest upon a conviction that any short-run danger lurks through such a move. The question is whether when circumstances turn difficult, the country will be in an equally solid position to maintain its growth if in the interim it has taken on a load of short-term debt and given investment banks the right to play games with its money. For example if, as some of us fear is quite likely, the US one day confronts a crisis caused by a collapse of the dollar, the consequence for the rest of the world is likely to be even more traumatic. Recession in the US will be tempered in the medium run by the shift in expenditure toward American-made goods caused by the dollar depreciation, but in other countries expenditure-switching and expenditure-reduction will reinforce each other in making for recession. Countries whose exchange rates float uncontrollably upwards will suffer the most. I am not for a moment suggesting that India should not be willing to play a role as a responsible member of the international community in accepting its fair share of the dollar depreciation, but simply that it would be advantageous to avoid the greater burden that might be thrust upon it by a market in which the free flow of capital dictates how far exchange rates move. And if India sought to maintain spending during a world recession through expansionary macroeconomic policies, it might well find that its reserves got run down even without a strong initial effective appreciation. At that point, the danger would be the more traditional one of a run out of the rupee.

I therefore see a series of reasons for India to take a go-slow approach in moving to liberalise the capital account. That it would be wise to liberalise one day I do not doubt. That there are some liberalising measures that should be made early—of FDI, of portfolio investment, of small private transactions—I find compelling. But there are many other liberalising reforms—from electricity pricing to making the courts work expeditiously to pruning the fiscal deficit—that deserve to be priorities over complete capital account liberalisation for the next 10 years (at least). At this stage full capital account liberalisation promises no large benefits, while it increases the risk of things going badly wrong.

FLAWED LOGIC OF CAPITAL ACCOUNT LIBERALISATION

Logic of Liberalisation

The government is exploring the possibility of further liberalising India's capital account. Despite limited and gradual liberalisation in the 1990s, for instance, relaxation of restrictions on foreign direct investment, allowing limited access for foreign institutional investors (FIIs) to the domestic capital market, and making restricted portfolio investment available to domestic and overseas corporate bodies and to non-resident Indians, numerous restrictions on capital flows are currently in force [Nayyar 2002]. Should the capital account be further liberalised?

The economic logic of the liberalisation of the capital account for less developed countries (LDCs) such as India (as distinct from merely "yielding" to pressure from western financial interests, or wanting India to graduate—prematurely—to the ranks of financially advanced nations) is related to the goals of increasing capital inflows in order to increase GDP and growth (and hence contribute to overall economic development) and of smoothing consumption through international borrowing.

The output-enhancing effect of capital account liberalisation can be seen from a simple textbook model in which one good is produced in two countries with two factors of production, "capital" and "labour", with given technology under conditions of diminishing returns to each factor. Suppose that the only difference between the two countries is that one—a developed country, DC—has a higher stock of capital than the other, an LDC. Under the assumption of perfect competition, but with labour and capital immobile between the two countries, the return to capital—or the rental rate—will be higher in the LDC than in the DC. If capital is allowed to move from the low-rental country to the high-rental country in search of higher returns, it will move from the rich country to the poor country, lowering its cost of capital, and adding to its production and income after paying the rental' to the rich country (also adding to world production and income, since capital has a higher marginal product in the LDC than in the DC). To the extent that the accumulation of capital leads to Higher growth such international capital flows increase growth in LDCs.

The consumption-stabilising impact can be shown with another simple model in which a country with a representative agent can borrow or lend at a given world interest rate. Suppose that the representative individual receives a stream of income which is subject to exogenous fluctuations. If consumption exhibits diminishing marginal utility, the individual (and country) will be able to increase its inter-temporal utility if it can participate in the international capital market and stabilise consumption.

Empirics of Liberalisation and International Capital Flows

Does empirical evidence confirm this logic of capital account liberalisation? A substantial increase in capital flows into emerging markets (consisting of LDCs and transitional economies) in the early and mid-1990s followed their capital market liberalisation. This phenomenon has been extensively studied and the evidence, which suggests that both arguments for capital account liberalisation are flawed, can be briefly summarised with four observations.

One, for reasonably long periods of time, and especially in recent years, there has been a reverse net transfer of financial resources from LDCs to rich countries. For instance, from 1997 onwards net transfers to LDCs have been negative, increasing from $5.2 billion in 1997 to over $350 billion in 2004, explained by a combination of low levels of net financial flows and the accumulation of foreign exchange reserves [Griffith-Jones, forthcoming].

Two, episodes of booms in capital inflows, especially short-term capital flows, end abruptly and turn into sharp outflows [Kaminsky, forthcoming].

Three, capital flows to emerging markets have been pro-cyclical, with large inflows during periods of economic expansion and outflows during recessions [Ocampo 2003; Kaminsky, forthcoming]. Further, fiscal and monetary policies tend to be pro-cyclical in LDCs and therefore exacerbate their business cycles.

Four, most episodes of interrelated banking and currency crises in emerging markets have been preceded by financial liberalisation and increased access to foreign capital markets [Kaminsky and Reinhart 1999].

These findings regarding capital market liberalisation and capital flows, especially portfolio investment and hot money flows, are well known and widely recognised. Bhagwati (2004), an avid defender of globalisation, warns about the perils of free international financial capital movements, and even the IMF has become less doctrinaire in supporting free movements of capital.

Imperfect Information, Uncertainty and Instability

Why is the logic of capital market liberalisation at odds with the actual experience of LDCs? It is flawed because it fails to come to grips with some fundamental features of reality of which the most important arguably relates to information.

Contrary to the assumption of perfect information in the standard model, information is imperfect in capital markets. Without deviating too much from the standard neoclassical assumption of optimising agents, models with asymmetric information produce results which are far more consistent with reality. If lenders do not know exactly what borrowers do with borrowed funds and can only observe cut comes of their activity, while borrowers know what they are doing, we have the problem of asymmetric information, and lenders will require collateral to ensure that borrowers do not willfully default. The implication of this that borrowers in rich countries who have higher initial endowments of capital will be able to borrow more than those in poor countries because they can put up collateral to overcome moral hazard problems, while borrowers in poor countries are less able to do so [Gertler and Rogoff 1990]. This may imply that capital will flow from poor to rich countries, making rich countries even richer, resulting in a process of uneven development.1 Borrowers in poor countries will not be able to borrow what they want to and will be rationed, and this rationing will become tighter when poor countries experience bad times, implying that capital flows to poor countries will be pro-cyclical and not stabilise their consumption.

Similar implications emerge from Keynes' (1936) view of asset markets in which investors are faced with fundamental uncertainty: they simply do not know the returns they can expect from their investments. In such a situation they form expectations of the future, knowing fully well that these expectations are built on flimsy foundations. In forming these expectations they may follow conventions, such as following the lead of others, which gives rise to herd mentality, and such conventions and expectations are likely to be subject to large changes in reaction to new information. At certain times business optimism is high, and that makes firms invest more, and this expansion results in an increase in aggregate demand which further fuels investment. This is possible because, unlike the neo-classical full employment model, the economy has unemployed resources. As the expansion proceeds, some firms may feel overextended and suddenly lose their confidence, and investment is curtailed, resulting in a reverse process of contraction and rising unemployment. Stock markets, in which asset holders try to guess what others believe, as in the famous beauty contest analogy, add to the instability.

Keynes' ideas have been extended and refined by post-Keynesian economists, most notably Minsky (1982), who analysed how the expectations of firms as borrowers and banks as lenders would change and interact. During the expansion firms borrow more and this leads them to become more indebted. Increased indebtedness leads lenders and borrowers to perceive greater risks, which induces lenders to increase the interest rate and borrowers to cut down on borrowing and investment. This decline in investment reduces aggregate demand in the standard Keynesian manner and results in a decline in profits which, along with the increase in interest rates leads to a downward spiral. Matters can be exacerbated when funds flow into real estate and stock markets. Herd mentality can lead to bubbles in these markets during the expansion, and when the bubbles inevitably burst, the price of assets (including those serving as collateral) tumble, which aggravates the financial positions of borrowers and lenders, leading to sharp reductions in lending and economic activity, as well as to bankruptcies. Keynes and Minsky were mainly discussing the financial markets within advanced capitalist economies, in which central banks can stabilise the economy, but matters are more complicated when we turn to international financial markets and LDCs.

Extending the analysis to international markets complicates matters for a number of reasons, including the following. First, the problems of uncertainty and asymmetric information are greater because market participants have less knowledge about situations and borrowers in distant countries. Lenders are therefore more likely to have their expectations built on flimsy foundations, exhibit more of a herd mentality, and rely more on conventions which are subject to sudden changes. Second, the fact that international markets operate with different currencies create additional sources of instability. During the boom, currency appreciation in borrower nations can lead to greater euphoria, and because loans have to be paid back in the currencies of lender nations, when loans are recalled during the downswing, currency depreciation can make it more difficult for borrowers to pay back loans. (Exchange rate fluctuations can in theory stabilise the market, but in practice have been found to amplify the lending cycles). Third, because of contagion effects across borders, for instance because foreign banks who suffer losses in one country can call back loans to another country, problems arising in one country can be transferred to other countries, introducing additional sources of instability. Fourth, since financial capital can move from one country to another, changes in the supply of finance to an economy can be greater than in a closed economy. Finally, the absence of a world central bank and the absence of monetary authorities that can regulate the amount of liquidity reduces the chances of containing the problem. In fact, the IMF, the closest thing to a world central bank, exacerbates the instability, deepening the bust by imposing austerity measures and other contractionary policies on borrowing countries, and by encouraging the imprudent lending boom by being ready to bail out lenders when financial crises occur.

LDCs are particularly prone to these problems while rich countries seldom experience currency crises. The small size of their financial markets-especially stock and currency markets—implies that a given change in capital flows has a large proportional effect on these markets. Poor prudential regulation and supervision of financial institutions, and the inexperience of financial agents in evaluating risks make them less able to reduce the instability of capital flows. Their thin securities markets reduce the ability of their monetary authorities to follow counter-cyclical policies which could dampen the fluctuations.

Consequences of Unstable Capital Flows

Unstable capital flows (although some components, such as foreign direct investment may be less unstable than others) can be expected to have adverse consequences on economic growth and social indicators in LDCs. The following discussion draws on available theoretical analysis and empirical investigations to present likely scenarios.

During the boom, private and public sector borrowing-financed expenditure increases [Ocampo 2003]. For the private sector, there may be some increase in real investment, but given that capital inflows are of short maturities, investments are more likely to be in the stock market and in real estate than in real capital formation [Demir 2005]. When interest rate spreads rise and credit is rationed and the bust occurs, the availability of funds falls, reducing investment and output.

The precise effects depend on the exchange rate regime. If the country has a flexible exchange rate, during the boom its currency will appreciate and this can affect growth adversely in a number of ways. If the economy is supply constrained, the decline in the profitability of the traded goods sector will shift resources to the non-traded sector, a shift which can slow down technological change if the traded goods sector has greater scope for learning by doing and has more technological externalities for other sectors. If the economy is aggregate demand-constrained, the reduction in net exports will result in a decline in aggregate demand, and hence output and investment and consequently, technological change driven by growth and investment. In either case, the result will be lower growth. The inflow of foreign capital is more likely to finance investments in stock markets and real estate than real capital formation, and the resultant asset price bubbles make real investment less attractive. Banks borrowing short abroad and lending long to firms for investment will also become fragile. When the bubble bursts and overextended lenders call back loans and capital leaves the country, the cost of borrowing for investment increases for firms and investment falls, as does output if it is constrainted by the availability of finance for working capital. The exchange rate depreciates, but this is unable to win back lost markets abroad because of hysteresis effect-kinked demand curves. Depreciation makes imported goods more expensive and thereby fuel inflation and if money wage are sticky this can result in a worsening of the income distribution. Depreciation also has a wealth effect, especially with currency mismatches, if loans have to be repaid in foreign currency and revenues are earned in domestic currency. All results in a downturn, which is exacerbated by cuts in government expenditure due to reduced access to credit and reduced revenue due to the downturn, which further reduces capital inflows.

If a country maintains a fixed exchange rate, or at least does not let the exchange rate float freely, capital inflows will result in the accumulation of foreign exchange reserves. Large foreign exchange reserves may serve to stabilise the currency and prevent outflows, but comes at the cost of holding low-return foreign assets as reserves which can lead to significant interest costs for the economy. Meanwhile, the credit boom spills over into financial markets and results in bubbles, and fails to increase capital formation. If the central bank leans against the wind and reduces domestic credit, this may fuel capital inflows by raising interest rates and further constrain investment. When the bubble bursts, there will be an outflow. The outflow will result in a contraction in money supply. Reserve losses of the central bank can lead to currency crises and the currency will have to be devalued and eventually floated, with the consequences discussed earlier.

The instability caused by capital flows further increases uncertainty and reduces investment. The resultant fall in output reduced external financing leads to cuts in government expenditure, especially in infrastructure and social programmes. The fall in employment and decline in government programmes increase poverty and a general deterioration in social indicators, unless expenditures are reallocated to the social sector [Taylor 2001].

2

Is Full Convertibility Possible in India?

India is debating whether to dismantle the remaining obstacles to full capital mobility. There are people, including this writer, who believe that this is fraught with dangers. But going by the actions of national governments, this view is clearly out of sync with the prevailing fashion. Among the developing (or emerging) countries today, only south Asia and China (with some other exceptions, e.g., Tanzania) have what is called a "repressed" or "partially repressed" capital account-actually India is classified by the International Monetary Fund as being "largely liberalised".

India is a latecomer to the debate involving capital account convertibility (indeed it is a latecomer to the whole set of macro-economic management issues) and there are benefits from learning about the advantages and pitfalls of having a more open capital account. The Asian crisis was a setback to those who believed that the markets should be given a free rein. These people are now back pointing to the mountain of foreign exchange that India is sitting on—a mere hillock compared to China and others in Asia—to make a case for immediate liberalisation of the capital account.

Our experience with unfettered capital mobility is recent. In the last quarter of a century there have been two peaks in net yearly private flows to developing or emerging countries. (I will use these expressions interchangeably.) The first peak of about $ 50 billion occurred in the early 1980s. The second peak of about $ 250 billion occurred just prior to the Asian crisis. Since then net flows to the emerging markets have trickled to zero or even turned negative—net transfers to Latin America including interest and profit repatriation are about minus $ 40 billion (India and China are exceptions). A worrying aspect of this drought is that it includes trade credit. One implication of this is that the positive aspect of a currency crisis, viz., a depreciation that used to stimulate exports, does not do so any more because of the paucity of trade credits.

The period is then too short for theorising on a grand scale—not that this has prevented anyone from doing so if they so wished. But there are some empirical regularities that one should bear in mind.

Broner and Rigobon (2004) analyse capital flows to 23 industrialised countries and 35 "emerging" countries—they looked at the capital account surplus for each country—using annual data over the period 1965-2003.[3] They found that the latter group has a standard deviation that is 1.8 times the former, and (left) skewness that is 1.5 times as much. They try to provide three sets of explanations: (a) the fundamentals may be different for the two groups; (b) the response to fundamentals may be different; and (c) non-fundamental shocks. The last set of factors includes "crises" or the role of outliers, "persistence" or the role of lags, and "contagion" or co-movement. They found that the third set of factors explain both the high variance and skewness, although country characteristics also matter.

Developing countries are told by mainstream economists to liberalise their trading regimes, and with some justification. Outward-looking economies (barring primary goods exporters) have done well from the GATT regime. Trade in goods at its crudest may be thought of as being timeless.

If the quality of goods is not an issue, then exchange can take place at any instant.

Should this enthusiasm for free trade carry over to trade in assets? At the level of an individual it is unfair that while a supplier may export a commodity and get a higher price abroad, a borrower should be prevented from accessing a supplier of loans abroad. Proponents of liberalisation of the capital account point to the opportunities for a small economy that the international market provides for diversification of idiosyncratic risk. Presumably, by holding a diversified portfolio one can buy insurance against country specific (temporary) shocks. Trade in asset markets inevitably involves time. Borrowing is to be repaid at a later date, etc. Contracts have to be written, issues of liquidity worked out. For the contracts to be enforceable, there has to be a legal authority, whose role is much more complex than one which might be checking on the quality of goods. Bankruptcy and the so-called inalienability of human capital only add to the complexity of the issues at hand. Underdeveloped countries with ill-functioning (or worse, non-existent) legal systems and thin (or worse, non-existent) markets need more care. Crony capitalism and asset price collapses are indicators of these—although on both counts Texas is also a candidate!

Historically, capital inflows to the colonies took the form of foreign direct investment (FDI) in mining and plantations and trade credits (where collateral is readily available). Also historically, trade credits (which are very short term) and FDI (which is long term) were both very stable components of capital flows. In the next historical episode, inflows took the form of syndicated bank loans to the government. It was much later that other forms of capital inflows, e.g., investment in equity, bank lending to the private sector, occurred. (This is the first peak in private flows mentioned earlier in the introduction.) The surge of capital inflows to the emerging economies which began in 1989 was supposed to be different from the one in the late 1970s in that in the previous episode almost all the lending was syndicated bank loans, whereas the later inflows were more diversified. One feature of a financial market that is not fully mature is that banking is the main form of financial intermediation. And since banks engage in maturity transformation, they are fragile (i.e., prone to crises). This is true of the rich countries as well. But they are able to cope with idiosyncratic shocks better since their production structure tends to be more diversified and banks constitute a smaller proportion of the financial sector. Given their underdeveloped financial markets, developing economies typically have (not unrealistically) a fear of outflow of capital if flows are liberalised. The two major types of outflows are: (i) capital flight: these may take place due to arbitrage opportunities presented by different tax rates for domestic residents and foreigners and in response to economic and political uncertainty; and (ii) outflows for portfolio diversification. Both kinds of outflows take place even in the presence of controls through a porous current account, through underinvoicing of exports and over in voicing of imports—for example, the errors and omissions in China's balance of payments statistics grew by $ 19.3 billion between 2002 and 2004 in anticipation of a revaluation of the RMB.4

Inflows and Outflows and Macroeconomic Performance

Capital account openness is supposed to provide a country with access to the international capital market and provide it with insurance. By way of an appetiser, I note that Caballero (2000) finds that for Chile—which is regarded as a resounding success story in terms of financial liberalisation—all the major macroeconomic series move, more or less, in tandem with the price of copper, which is Chile's main export.

Capital inflows of all kinds, following liberalisation, generate an appreciation of the real exchange rate. These squeeze the domestic tradeables sector, which would put the whole liberalisation process at risk. Also, if the financial system is not developed this gives rise to a lending boom (through, e g, implicit guarantees to foreign capital).5 This overtime leads to losses on loans. If a stock market boom, as in India in recent times, led to investment and real growth, it would be welcome. What happens, more often than not, is that a consumption boom occurs with the party ending with the inevitable outflow. So, some form of capital controls helps provide time for the domestic financial sector to prepare for the challenge of opening up.

Outflows leave individuals and banks with foreign currency denominated liabilities—hedging is not well developed and is simply unable to cope with a system-wide crisis. In the wake of the outflow, interest rates rise and the currency depreciates. These put further strain on the financial sector. The positive aspects of a currency depreciation in raising exports needs, as mentioned earlier, trade credits.

Among the capital account items, FDI is more stable and it provides new technology and creates jobs—not all of FDI does this, but the bulk of these flows do. It is portfolio and bank lending that constitute a problem. FDI and portfolio investment flows are not correlated. Among the developing counties, China is the single-largest recipient of FDI—its capital account was quite closed till recently—while Brazil was the largest recipient of portfolio investment.

In east Asia, bank lending, which constituted an inflow of $ 114 billion in 1996 turned into an outflow of $ 54 billion in 1998, the figure for 2000 being an outflow of $ 13 billion. Portfolio investment declined from $ 17 billion to $ 5 billion. Similarly, in Latin America, between 1996 and 1999, bank loans fell from $ 49 billion to $7 billion. For all emerging markets between 1996 and 2000, bank loans fell from being about 56 per cent of all inflows to about a fifth of all inflows.

Countries which have restricted the flow of capital have used two broad types of capital control mechanisms: (a) one which distinguishes between transactions—implemented, e.g., in Chile and Argentina (where there are some items that remain closed to all market participants), and (b) one which differentiates between domestic residents and others, with domestic residents being forbidden from participating in certain transactions—almost inevitably this translates into liberalising inflows first, and then outflows. This is the strategy followed in India am South Africa.

When Is Full Convertibility Possible?

There are three prerequisites for liberalising the capital account highlighted in the literature: (a) financial sector reforms, (b) fiscal balance; and (c) properly designed monetary (and exchange rate; policy. But as pointed out by Griffith-Jones, Williamson and Gottschalk (2005). It is the absence of these factors but with the presence of capital flows that an external crisis occurs. For instance, India had a weak banking system and so did Thailand. But India was not affected by the Asian crisis.

Financial Sector Reforms

Financial sector reforms can be painful even in the absence of capital flows. To absorb capital inflows, most of which tend to be short-term, what is needed is a strong domestic financial system resilient enough to cope with inflows and outflows. A movement away from quantitative restrictions to more market determined interest rates, prudential norms, development of a money market, markets for government securities, and foreign exchange, the existence of a yield curve for pricing floating rate instruments, etc, are required to be in place. The Basel prudential norms, which have been criticised (correctly) for other reasons, have helped set some standards in the banking sector. In addition to currency mismatch there could also be maturity mismatch. It is only after financial liberalisation that the banking sector's non-performing assets (NPAs) have been recognised as a problem—in the past they were just swept under the carpet. The definition, provisioning, etc, are norms that are still evolving in developing economies.

As mentioned above, bank credit tends to grow quickly following an inflow of capital. This leads to funding of high-risk projects and because of the inadequate monitoring and information the banks' balance sheets become strained. Excessive risk taking is more likely in a regime where there are implicit or explicit government guarantees. In these situations it is important that banks should not have access to foreign borrowing, because excessive lending takes place without adequate monitoring or hedging of foreign currency.

Corrective action takes place only after a crisis erupts, as in Thailand. The Thai banking crisis, which heralded the Asian crisis in 1997, is widely believed to be due to poor monitoring by the Thai central bank. About half of the (unhedged) foreign exchange loans were made to firms located in the non-traded goods sector.

Monetary (and Exchange Rate) Policy

Fiscal and monetary policies have to ensure that volatility of capital flows is minimised. Low inflation, budget balance and an independent central bank are prerequisites for such a policy. Foreign capital inflows may cause additional headaches for the monetary authorities. First, they may want to sterilise the effects of the flows on money supply to prevent changes in the money stock, which are pro-cyclical. This may be done through the usual channels of monetary policy, though for an economy, which is financially integrated with the rest of the world, the cash reserve ratio (CRR) cannot be too much out of line with the levels abroad. Second, the authorities may conduct an open market operation. This requires some depth in financial markets, which may be missing. Sterilisation through this route may have budgetary implications because now the government, by engaging in it, places in the hands of the public an interest-bearing liability in place of cash. A third alternative is to target a segment of the flows directly. Chile (also Colombia and Thailand) has had some success in transforming the maturity of capital flows through an 'encaje' or unremunerated reserve requirement (URR) but whether there was any effect of this on total flows is doubtful.

Exchange rate flexibility is also necessary. Much has been written on the impossibility of maintaining free mobility of capital, fixed exchange rates and an independent monetary policy—the impossible trinity. A regime of flexible exchange rates has its drawbacks but is clearly preferable to a fixed exchange rate regime in a situation where capital account convertibility is being contemplated. Fixed exchange rates do not allow for inflation differentials, convert returns into foreign currencies one-for-one and are prone to one-way bets against the central bank. In the recent past most developing countries have switched to a floating exchange rate system. Malaysia is still on a fixed exchange rate regime—it had also imposed temporary capital controls—while Argentina was on a currency board till recently.

There is an even bigger argument against a fixed exchange rate regime in developing economies, especially with implicit guarantees: it causes inflows with the borrowing denominated in the foreign currency, which may then be lent to the non-traded goods sector. If it looks as if an exchange rate crisis could occur, market participants move out of the domestic currency (a one way bet causes a run on the foreign exchange reserves of the central bank), which may cause the fixed exchange rate regime to collapse. The collapse makes the domestic banks vulnerable to a crisis because their balance sheets deteriorate in terms of the foreign currency (domestic currency loans especially those to the non-traded goods sector fall in value). This is what happened in Thailand and Indonesia. The central bank may try to protect the peg by raising interest rates. This may cause fragile businesses to go under and thus worsen the banks' balance sheets further (see Mishkin (1999) for a discussion).

One justification, often overlooked, for some form of a pegged rate is that capital flows are prone to reversals—there was the debate mentioned above about whether capital flows are caused by pull factors (i.e., country-specific performance) or push factors (OECD business cycle, interest rates, etc). If indeed a reversal of a capital flow is likely, then with some nominal wage-price inertia it may be optimal not to have a floating exchange rate regime. A floating exchange rate regime would cause an immediate real appreciation and a current account deficit, the output and employment costs of these could be substantial. With a pegged exchange rate system, on the other hand, the overvaluation occurs gradually over time. It is very difficult for the authorities, given the few episodes of international capital flows, to decide whether the shock (i.e., the inflow of capital) is permanent or temporary and therefore what the appropriate policy response should be.

A hard-peg (e.g., a currency board), which for many analysts was the favourite form of a nominal anchor, has become less fashionable. It involved surrendering discretionary monetary policy altogether. Its fall from grace is due to Argentina tying its fortunes to the US dollar. Having tied its own hand it suffered the consequences of a strong dollar and an inflexible labour market. To see why just compare the recent experience of Brazil, which has a floating rate and Argentina, which had a currency board (this is equally true of Hong Kong versus the rest of east Asia). Some form of nominal exchange rate fixing—with the currency board as an extreme form—pays rich dividends in bringing down inflation in countries prone to high (or hyper) inflation. It is a good idea, however, to move to a floating regime once this has been achieved. But what is the correct time to dismount the tiger of "credibility"?

Fiscal Policy

The government's fiscal stance is also important for a successful liberalisation of the capital account. If there is a large budget deficit (or more correctly debt) then the real interest rate will tend to be high, attracting inflows. This will cause a real appreciation, which with a floating rate could be achieved through a nominal appreciation. In the presence of fixed exchange rates this inflow could cause an increase in the nominal money supply and generate inflationary pressures. To sterilise the money supply the central bank could conduct an open market operation, which, as noted above, requires some depth in these markets. But even a sterilisation operation is only a temporary fix because, as mentioned in the previous sub-section, this increases the government debt held by residents and hence adds to the interest cost.10 In any case the tradeables sector, which was being squeezed before capital mobility was allowed, is hurt even more. This could make the current account deficit unsustainable. In anticipation of such an eventuality, a reversal of capital flows could take place. Brazil was able to attract a lot of foreign portfolio capital in the early 1990s. But the government's (both federal and provincial) deficits were sizeable.

It should be noted that prudent fiscal behaviour by itself is not enough to keep as crisis at bay. After all, most of the southeast Asian countries had "reasonable" deficits and contagion tends not to discriminate between those who are well behaved and those who are not. But the experience of Argentina, Chile and Uganda shows that with the government deficit under control the financial system can handle inflows better, and as mentioned above, in Brazil fiscal profligacy did lead to a crisis.

In conclusion, one can say that a strong financial sector is required if a nation is to reap the potential gains from trade in assets. Even to benefit from trade in goods, some sectors are expected to contract, while others expand. In the financial markets, the collapse of a few institutions could lead to a collapse of the entire financial system. The experience of emerging economies suggests that one should approach the issue of throwing open the capital account with extreme caution.

3

Emerging Issues of Currency Sovereignty and Policy Independency

This essay examines the benefits of currency sovereignty, defined as a floating exchange rate currency issued by a sovereign government. This arrangement provides both fiscal and monetary policy independence, allowing a government to pursue domestic policy goals such as full employment. Note that there are differing degrees of currency independence. Some nations drop their currencies altogether and adopt a foreign currency for use in the domestic economy. Dollarisation is an example. Others continue to use their own currency, but fix it to a foreign currency. So long as a 100 per cent cover of the foreign currency is held on reserve (official deposits at the foreign central bank, or securities issued by the foreign treasury), there is no important difference between this and "dollarisation" (since in both cases governments must have the dollars needed to cover government liabilities). This is essentially how Argentina's currency board operated holding dollar reserves on a one-to-one basis against pesos issued and promising to convert pesos to dollars on demand. Still others peg the exchange rate to a foreign currency, but hold less than 100 per cent reserve backing. In practice, this is a very risky proposition if the exchange rate is fixed and conversion on demand is permitted. Hence, the behaviour of a prudent government operating with less than 100 per cent reserves would not be much different from one operating with 100 per cent reserves, because any policy that might provoke a "run" on the currency would force it to default on its promise to convencies Even a 100 per cent reserve backing w not be sufficient if the government issues non-money liabilities (for example, treasury securities) to borrow dollars. As result, countries that peg their currency also constrain "capital flows" by limiting currency conversion and imposing other capital controls, and by trying to achieve a current account surplus. This in turn generally means domestic policy is biased toward austerity: high interest rates (attract capital flows) and fiscal restraint (to keep inflation and imports low because policy must focus on maintain!] the exchange rate, it subordinates other policy goals – most importantly, full employment and domestic growth and development.

We will first examine Argentina's experience with a currency board that led a crisis. We then analyse in detail why currency sovereignty generates the conditions required for policy independence We will see how Argentina in the after math of crisis put in place policies that allowed it to recover, concluding with implications for India.

Argentina's Experience with a Currency Board

In 1991, Argentina adopted a currency board based on the dollar—a last ditch effort to constrain inflation. From that point forward it surrendered currency sovereignty as it became a user of a currency rather than an issuer. The creation of the currency board, as well as various structural reforms that included rapid privatisation of state assets and downsizing of the national government did appear to bring major benefits. Exports plus imports as a per cent of GDP grew well over 7 per cent annually during the first half of the 1990s, boosted by US demand, as the economy was opened and trade was liberalised. Federal expenditures fell from more than 27 per cent of GDP at the end of the 1980s to about 20 per cent during the 1990s; the federal budget achieved a balance during the first half of the 1990s (even a surplus in 1994). Inflation fell from nearly 100 per cent at the beginning of the 1990s to nearly zero for the rest of the decade (until the currency board collapsed). It is no wonder that those who promoted the Washington Consensus viewed Argentina's experiment as a nearly unqualified success.

The problem was that the policy package lent a slow-growth bias to the economy by constraining fiscal policy. Unemployment remained high, and inequality rose, throughout the currency board experiment. Growth relied on non-governmental spending—either domestic consumption and investment or a trade surplus. However, pegging to the dollar made Argentinian exports less competitive whenever its competitors devalued. Dollar and, thus, peso appreciation caused imports to rise more quickly than exports so that a persistent trade deficit arose after 1992. With a trade deficit, Argentina could obtain needed dollars only by borrowing or by selling assets. Moreover, as deflationary forces built up (with negative inflation-adjusted GDP growth every year from 1999 onwards), tax revenue growth fell off so that the federal government began to run a persistent deficit by the mid-1990s, and provincial governments (and the private sector) accumulated big debts.

In an attempt to slow the growth of its own deficits, the federal government cut transfers to regional governments, forcing them to downsize. This constrained growth of income and private spending, which further eroded tax revenues, eventually brought regional governments to the edge of default. Interestingly, regional governments experimented with novel financing methods, paying with short-term debt that they then accepted in payment of regional taxes. The 'patacones' were—one example, and were soon accepted all over the country (even for utility company payments and for Big Macs at McDonald's!), and eventually were accepted by the national government in payment of taxes. However, for regional governments these only temporarily averted default—since at maturity they were supposed to be redeemed for pesos, making them additional peso debt for the provinces. And for me nations! government they actually hastened default since they reduced peso and dollar revenue as citizens chose to pay taxes in patacones.

Additionally, since Argentinian interest rates did not fall as expected (indeed, its interest rates remained on par with those of its neighbours after creation of the currency board, indicating that market assessment of default risk substituted nearly perfectly for reduced currency risk), federal debt service payments grew fairly rapidly (by 2000, interest costs alone were about 17 per cent of national government pending). Hence, the combination of slow Economic growth and high government narrowing rates ensured a vicious cycle of pressures on the treasury to increase fiscal austerity, which hindered growth, raised unemployment, and increased fiscal pressures as taxable income fell. Federal governmental default was inevitable, as was the extreme social unrest that normally comes when unemployment reaches 20 per cent.

In conclusion, even if it is accepted that dollarisation brought initial benefits, to put Argentina in an unsustainable situation. The whole package came crashing down by Christmas 2001 as Argentina defaulted on its dollar debts, abandoned the currency board, refused to convert pesos to dollars, and floated the currency. Street protests brought down a series of governments. However, little more than a year later, Argentina began to mount a strong recovery. This was accomplished by the combination of floating the currency, defaulting on external dollar debt payments, and creating a job guarantee. We will return to the successful implementation of this package of policies after examining in detail how sovereign currencies work.

Currency Sovereignty

A nation like the US (as well as countries like Japan and Turkey, and Argentina after it abandoned the currency board) creates a currency for domestic use (and ensures its use primarily by demanding payment of taxes in that currency, although some go further by adopting legal tender laws). The government, itself (including the treasury and the central bank—the Fed in the case of the US), issues and spends high powered money (HPM—cash and reserves at the central bank) as its liability. The US government does not promise to ^ convert its HPM to any other currency, nor to gold or any other commodity, at any fixed exchange rate. The flexible exchange rate is key to maintaining fiscal and currency independence—what I call sovereignty, although governmental sovereignty certainly has other dimensions as well. But there is more to it than a flexible exchange rate. The sovereign government spends (buys goods, services, or assets, or makes transfer payments) by issuing a treasury cheque, or, increasingly, by simply crediting a private bank deposit. In either case, however, credit balances (HPM) are created when the central bank credits the reserve account of the receiving bank. Analogously, when the government receives tax payments, it reduces the reserve balance of a bank. Simultaneously, the taxpayer's bank deposit is debited. While we commonly think of a government needing to first receive tax revenue, and then spending that revenue, this sequence is not necessary for any sovereign government. If a government spends by crediting a bank account (issuing its own IOU—HPM) and taxes by debiting a bank account (and eliminating its IOU—HPM), then it is not as a matter of logic, "spending" tax revenue. In other words, with a floating exchange rate and a domestic currency, the sovereign government's ability to make payments is neither revenue-constrained nor reserve-constrained.

This fundamentally simple point is difficult for some to grasp because we are used to thinking about government as if it were not sovereign. It is the non-sovereign government that must obtain money before it can spend; for the most part, it obtains money by taxing and borrowing (governments also sell services, assets, and seme commodities to obtain money). For example, state governments in the US are non-sovereign in the sense in which I am using the term. They really do spend tax revenue. When state taxes are paid, bank deposits of taxpayers are debited and those of the state governments are credited. These governmental deposits are then used when state governments spend, leading to debits to their accounts and credits to the accounts of those receiving state government cheques. When tax revenues fall, states have to cut spending, raise taxes, or borrow to finance their spending. However, state borrowing is ultimately limited by market assessment of default risk. Thus, states are forced to act in a pro-cyclical manner in recession, cutting spending and raising taxes and thereby exacerbating the unemployment problems.

In the US it is the federal government (the sovereign) that ultimately has the responsibility and the means to maintain full employment—not the individual, non-sovereign states. Logically, this is implied by the fiscal arrangements. As the sovereign issuer of the currency, only the national government is able to spend without regard to revenue. Fiscal transfers (mostly from the US treasury, although the Fed can also play a role) from Washington to the states can help counter the pro-cyclical behaviour of states. Note that when Argentina adoptee the currency board, it put itself into: situation that is much like that of US states If Washington had stepped in to provide sufficient transfers to the non-sovereign Argentina, it could have prevented a f fiscal economic, and social crisis. Unfortunately such a policy would have had little political support in the US.

When a household or non-sovereign government borrows, it issues an IOU and obtains a bank deposit that it needs in order to spend. The sovereign government, on the other hand, has no need I obtain a deposit before it spends its own currency, crediting a private bank account. It sells a security, not to finance paying expenditures but to reduce the out standing stock of HPM, merely offering to substitute one of its interest-paying liabilities (the security) for a non-interest-paying liability (the HPM that is debited fro bank accounts). This is really an interest rate management operation (known with the US Federal Reserve as offsetting operating factors)—reducing bank reserves in order to eliminate (non-interest-earning) excess reserves that would otherwise place downward pressure overnight interest rates.

The final point is that the interest rate paid on sovereign securities is not subject to normal "market forces". The sovereign government only sells securities in on to drain excess reserves to hit its inter rate target. It could always choose to simply leave excess reserves in the banking system in which case the overnight rate would toward zero. When the overnight rat zero, the treasury can always offer to securities that pay a few basis poi above zero and will find willing buy because such securities offer a be return than the alternative (zero) drives home the point that a severe government with a floating currency issue securities at any rate it desire normally a few basis points above overnight interest rate target it has There may well be economic or political reasons for keeping the overnight above zero (which means the inte rate paid on securities will also be at zero), but it is faulty reasoning that leads to the belief that the size of a sovereign government deficit affects the interest rate paid on securities.

For a real world example, one need only look at the current case of Japan, which has long had the largest government deficit (relative to GDP—reaching to 8 per cent) as well as the all-time largest outstanding government stock of debt (over 150 per cent of GDP) of any major developed country. However, Japan long maintained interest rates on government securities at a few basis points above zero (and sometimes, for technical reasons, even below zero!). It recently announced that it will finally raise rates above zero—as a policy, not as something imposed upon it by markets. The US accomplished the same feat during the second world war, when short-term treasuries paid 3/8th of 1 per cent even as the deficit-to-GDP ratio reached 25 per cent of GDP—three times higher than Japan's current ratio! This indicates that a sovereign nation with a floating exchange rate can choose interest rates on government debt as low as it wants. By the same token, the sovereign government could have interest rates above 100 per cent if it so desired. All it needs to do is set the overnight rate target at 100 per cent and then sell securities whenever excess reserves placed downward pressure on that rate. This drives home the point that the interest rate is exogenously set in any sovereign nation. Whether the base rate will be zero or 100 is a monetary policy matter, not subject to market determination.

A non-sovereign government faces an entirely different

situation. In the case of a "dollarised" nation, the government must obtain dollars before it can spend them. Hence, it uses taxes and issues IOUs to obtain dollars in anticipation of spending; unlike the case of a sovereign nation, this government must have "money in the bank" (dollars) before it can spend. Further, in contrast to the sovereign nation, the non-sovereign government promises to deliver third party IOUs (that is, dollars) to service its own debt (while the US and other sovereign nations promise only to deliver their own IOUs). Because of this, the interest rate on the non-sovereign, dollarised government's liabilities is not independently set (whether it is a US state or an Argentina). Since it is borrowing dollars, the rate it pays is determined by two factors. First, there is the base rate on dollars set by the monetary policy of the US (the issuer of the dollar). On top of that is the market's assessment of the non-sovereign government's credit-worthiness. A large number of factors may go into determining this assessment. The important point, however, is that the non-sovereign government, as user (not issuer) of a currency cannot independently set the interest rate. Rather, market forces determine the interest rate at which it borrows.

Implications of Currency Sovereignty

When Argentina abandoned the currency board, it gained policy independence: its exchange rate was no longer tied to the dollar's performance. Its fiscal policy was no longer held hostage to the quantity of dollars the government could accumulate and its domestic interest rate came under control of its central bank. One of the first policy initiatives taken by newly elected president Nestor Kirchner was a job creation programme that guaranteed employment for poor heads of households. Within four months, the'Plan Jefes y Jefas de Hogar' had created jobs for two million participants—equal to 13 per cent of the labour force. This not only helped to quell social unrest by providing income to Argentina's poorest families, but it also put the economy on the road to recovery. Conservative estimates of the multiplier effect of the increased spending by'Jefes' workers are that it added a boost of more than 2.5 per cent of GDP. In addition, the programme provided needed services and new public infrastructure that encouraged additional private sector spending. Without the flexibility provided by a sovereign, floating, currency, the government would not have been able to promise such a job guarantee.

Argentina also benefited from currency flexibility that was made possible by dropping the peg to the dollar, as her exports became competitively priced. The US expansion as well as the worldwide rise of commodity prices have helped Argentinian exports. To be sure, there is some precariousness inherent in reliance on export-led growth. Argentina realises it must also continue to develop its domestic markets so that it won't be so reliant on US growth. Currency sovereignty allows the nation to use fiscal policy (and monetary policy) to continue to create jobs in the private and public sectors.

Like Argentina, India is enjoying rapid growth of GDP, currently fuelled by favourable export conditions. India is also in the process of implementing a limited job guarantee, in part to deal with very uneven economic performance across regions. However, resolving India's unemployment and poverty problems may require a greater fiscal commitment than its government is prepared to undertake. India is rightly concerned with the financial and exchange rate crises suffered nor long ago by Asian and Latin American nations, triggered by large external debts, declining foreign currency reserves, and market expectations that exchange rate pegs could not be held. However, it must be recognised that these nations had adopted (formal or informal) pegs to the dollar. By contrast, a nation that adopts its own floating rate currency can always afford to put unemployed domestic resources to work. Its government will issue liabilities denominated in its own currency, and will service its debt in its own currency. Whether its debt is held internally or externally, it faces no insolvency risk. Further, the floating currency gives domestic policy an additional degree of freedom. This does not mean that the nation will necessarily ignore its trade balance or movements of its exchange rate, but it does mean that it can put domestic employment and growth at the top of its policy agenda.

4

Capital Movements in Some Countries

On December 21, 2001, barely three days before Christmas, the holiest of all festivities in a predominantly Catholic country, when people normally go on a spending spree to exchange gifts, monetary havoc was bestowed on a country already suffering two years of a deep downturn and many more of fiscal retrenchment. The unthinkable happened: the vast majority of Argentinians were denied the money they rightfully held.

Every first year undergraduate taking a macroeconomics course knows that the narrowest definition of money comprises banknotes and deposits on current accounts with the commercial banking system. Money is a monetary institution's liability that can be legally claimed on demand in exchange for central bank money, the prime means of transaction and legal tender of which banks must hold sufficient reserves. On that fatal and beleaguered day, Argentinians were hot on their heels to rush to their banks' counters to claim back their current account deposits. There was an extraordinary reason. Normally, if current account holders lose trust in their banks and claim central bank money, the former can draw on their reserves, and if in want of these, the latter can always issue, albeit in distress, further balances to rescue them or to force them to fail with as little harm to the public as possible. But Argentinians had a further legal claim: the law allowed them to trade in their peso balances in exchange for US dollars at the central bank, on request. In the, weeks preceding that day, rumours had spread, and in the early hours it had become a certainty that the central bank was not in a position to honour its legal liability. As a consequence, the exchange rate, that had been kept fixed for a decade, was to be devalued by a large amount. Everybody ran for his or her money, but there was not enough.

Political Backdrop and Economic Theory

The end of the 1980s had brought with it the scorching experience of soaring inflation; it was, in fact, a hyperinflation that had reached the mind-boggling rate of 5,000 per cent on a yearly basis. It was an excruciatingly painful event that threatened to, and indeed did, gnaw into people's purchasing power. Life was turned into a bitter struggle in which everybody tried to scrape his or her way to relative safety by seeking a hedge to safeguard daily income as best as they could. Prices increased sizeably from morning to evening and no one could be sure that his or her real income would be maintained; everybody had literally become a speculator in search of protection through anything that could be reputed a viable alternative to holding money balances. Inflation had to be tamed if the country were to remain a democracy. The memory and legacy of the military junta with its trail of human tragedies were still fresh and temptations to settle political and social problems by a coup d'etat, a frequent occurrence in Argentina, still ran high when president Raoul Alfonsin met his demise, shifting executive power to Carlos Menem, a poncho wearing, long sideburned chieftain from the distant sub-Andean province of La Rioja. Menem was a member of Peron's Justicialista Party. Yet, whilst he stuck to the traditional populist rhetoric, he embraced ultraliberal, right wing policies, supported by much of the predominant theory. This attitude needs some explaining.

It may possibly be rather glib to assess the full extent of US ideology and cultural ascendancy on the Latin American ruling elites and upon public opinion in general, but it is certainly an undisputed fact that nowhere else in the whole world did the assertions and prescriptions of the so-called Chicago school of economics gain such a deep root as amongst Argentinian academics and policy-makers. Some observers have gone as far as stating that it was the presumed and debatable success of the economic advisors to Chile's Augusto Pinochet, many of whom took wide renown as the "Chicago boys", that firmly established the doctrine as a benchmark of excellent theory and crucial reference for policy-making. Basically, the following are the tenets of the theory that became widely accepted political currency, especially after Menem took office.

(1) An economy that is unfettered by harmful barriers, policy-created hurdles and distorting laws tends to an equilibrium of real magnitudes and relative prices that are the true economy's fundamentals and that cannot be upset by fiddling with nominal aggregates.

(2) This strong result rests on far-fetched assumptions attributing to economic agents Olympian capabilities, with rational expectations that eschew all radical uncertainty, implying, on average, near perfect knowledge of the true model of how the economy works.

(3) The implication is that government policies cannot modify the underlying fundamental equilibrium, but cause temporary yet upsetting perturbations.

(4) Investment flows are governed by relative prices, the profit rate and the interest rate.

In a truly market driven environment, financial capital and' goods flow freely in and out of a country determining an equilibrium exchange rate. Any trade deficit is automatically a capital surplus. In this context, monetary policy and demand management must only accommodate growth, but in no case steer the economy away from its natural path and its natural rate of unemployment and natural activity level, since rational expectations forestall, aside from temporary oscillations, attempts to veer-away from fundamental equilibrium. Policy tools that interfere directly with supposedly smoothly working markets such as sectorally targeted industrial and credit policies, and subsidies, even if directed to the very poor, should be banned from the dictionary of policy-making.

We must now dwell on what this meant in Argentina in the decade of the 1990s. By following this orthodox prescription, capital movements were allowed to flow unhindered in and out of the country, given that they were assumed to merely chase the best profit opportunities. Accordingly, a balance of payments current account deficit was thought to matter little if not at all in this context since, provided that the interest rate were a market rate orienting investment opportunities, it would neatly be offset by an equal amount of capital inflows. Thus, the exchange rate would not be perturbed by a trade imbalance. Subsidies and government provided incentives rapidly became blasphemous swearwords and their supporters were treated with haughty contempt by those, having studied in the seminaries of orthodox theory, claimed to know better. This view contrasts, of course, even with the less fundamentalist neoclassical views, according to which imperfectly functioning markets, asymmetries of information and less than perfect foresight make current account deficits and debt stock signposts of the path that the exchange rate is likely to follow.

Why in Argentina?

One may wonder why it is that such a theory became the leading beacon of so much policy-making in a country like Argentina. Whilst academics were under the spell of Nobel Prize winning theorists and saw it as a great intellectual challenge of being able to follow in the foot steps of world acclaimed economists and a key to a bright university career, it is less obvious why an entire society accustomed more to populist politicking and to bartering votes for patronage would accept the rigour of a highly constrained ultra liberal policy. The explanation lies with the inflationary process that plagued the country in the aftermath of the military dictatorship and that had bored deeply into the trust and certainties of the vast majority of the population.

Policies in the 1990s

When he was elected, president Menem was widely considered by many to be the clan head of a province where political horse-trading and widespread corruption were the norm. In spite of this very traditional and century honoured habits, he called upon a Harvard trained economist, Domingo Cavallo, to tame the four digit inflation that had ridden the country for several years. The most important measure in the policy packet that was introduced soon after his inauguration was the so-called convertibility law ('Ley de Convertibilitad'). This law reintroduced the peso and commanded an irrevocably fixed exchange rate of one Argentinian peso for one US dollar. Cavallo was well aware that legislating a fixed exchange rate meant nothing without the backing of necessary rules constraining monetary authorities. To ensure that this was indeed the case, the law mandated the central bank of Argentina to convert on demand any amount of pesos into dollars. In practice, if the latter was to have sufficient backing for the peso quantity of money in circulation, it had to keep a nearly equal amount of dollar reserves. Argentina, had, therefore, chosen a currency board and relinquished its monetary sovereignty. What the law implied was that the growth of the money supply was to be entirely determined by the net inflow of capital, boosting the financial systems holdings of dollar reserves. This meant that the central bank was to monitor the reference interest rate in order to keep it aligned with the US Federal rate plus, it is important to note, the perceived country risk. Hence, it is true to say that the peso was almost equivalent to the US dollar but not quite the same: the degree to which they actually differed could be measured by agents' evaluation of the risk of holding peso denominated liabilities. It also meant that the central bank had to strictly monitor the trading and commercial banks' reserve requirement in order to keep the overall quantity of money redeemable in US currency on demand This, in turn, meant seeing to it that deposits on current account and their endogenous determination through bank credit were kept strictly within the closed bounds of a credit multiplier not very different from one.

It is important to stress that an effective currency board, especially if the anchor currency is an international reserve currency, requires unfettered capital movements. Thus, the growth of the money supply depends on the net inflow of anchor denominated capital and on the reserve currency country's monetary policy. Since the latter was the US, this also depends on the willingness of the US Federal Reserve system to render liquidity available to the domestic and international markets. It is also important to remark that this dependency, although less binding than in the case, of a stiff currency board, also applies to economies allowing free capital movements. In a world where there are very few recognised reserve currencies, it is the latter that set the reference real rate of interest thus constraining all other currencies to comply if the exchange rate is to remain relatively stable. In turn, this constraint is more or less binding according to how financial markets form their expectations. Without resorting to any strong rational expectation assumptions, it seems to be a fairly well established fact that operators do target some fundamental benchmark to, forecast the likely behaviour of a given currency. As the 1997 east Asian crisis has shown, debt growth, especially the short-term one, and the current account deficit that feeds it may likely rouse devaluation expectations and thus capital flight leading to an actual devaluation. In this context, the real exchange rate that is judged to maintain balance becomes another constraint for a free capital movement economy, whence the requirement that the rate of inflation be kept fairly strictly within the range of the one prevailing in the reserve currency country. This is why wage moderation and less intrusive trade unions are often advocated to discipline such an economy, implying' a trade off between international discipline and policy sovereignty.

The Menem government made sure that capital movements were indeed free to move. Markets were liberalised and most state owned companies were sold, mostly to foreign firms, especially to Spanish interests following the neo-Atlantic mood taken by Spain towards its erstwhile overseas colonies. This outright sale took place by under pricing assets, thanks to kickbacks that are still being investigated by Argentinian courts. All industrial policies were scrapped, subsidies cut back and public expenditure restructured in favour of patronage and against public utilities: schools and public universities, for example, were starved of funds whilst letting their private counterparts flourish.

Consequences

Inflation was stopped abruptly. The change over to the new currency was quite smooth, even if real adjustment had been severe. In 1992-93, inflation was a thing of the past. Had policies changed then and become less rigid, Argentina might have been spared the tragedy that was to come. Yet, apparent good results, academic pressure to pursue orthodox recipes and, above all, the interests of rent-seeking classes of societies who thrived on overvalued financial wealth conjured to convince the Menem government to stick to its one peso one dollar currency board policy. Its dire consequences showed up without delay: an overvalued peso caused a deficit in the trade balance and then in the current account that mounted year after year, according to a very predictable time pattern. Manufacturing industries became non-competitive and thus pushed out of international markets, especially those with neighbouring 'Mercosur' countries and, above all, with the major trade partner, Brazil. The only sectors that remained competitive were resource based, normally capital intensive industries that were the main actors on international dollar priced markets and many of which had been purchased by foreign corporations. Yet, not even the capital inflows generated by the latter were sufficient to offset the deficit implied borrowing requirement. As long as interest rates remained high enough to cover a slowly increasing country risk, foreign capital kept entering Argentina's financial system. This fact was seen as a triumph of the market principle. In the first part of the 1990s growth remained buoyant, led first by pent up consumption spending and then by an inter-industry restructuring away from manufactures to the benefit of Financial, service and resource based sectors. Productivity statistics were excellent but concealed the fact that much of the growth was actually due to the closing down of many manufacturing firms whose efficiency, if measured by international standards, was less than good and that had been able to survive under the protection of high tariffs. Nevertheless, these firms were the backbone of Argentina's industrial sector, provided a large share of overall employment and were the custodians of considerable technological capabilities, skills and know-how. They had a problem, of course, but the problem was of enhancing their performance and bringing them up to the standards of international competitiveness, not to close them outright. There were two indicators, however, that told a different story. The first was seen as a mild puzzle: the rate of unemployment never dropped, even in the years of high growth, below 14-15 per cent. The second was almost entirely ignored: the Gini coefficient measuring inequality steadily grew across social classes and between thriving urban and decaying provincial populations. This outcome of Menem's policy stance could have been entirely foreseen. There was, indeed, a major flaw even with the currency board chosen. If one has to be chosen for any period of time it is crucial to determine the country's trade orientation and the pattern of direct investment flows that are likely to bolster capital movements. This is clearly very important since if the domestic currency must follow the ups and downs of its anchor, it must not lose competitiveness in relation to trade partners lest the current account start to generate offsetting debt. This was clearly never the case for Argentina, given that its major trading partner within Mercosur was and still is Brazil, a country that had chosen a flexible exchange rate policy, and that the one outside was Europe. Thus, in spite of a very low inflation rate, when during the decade of the 1990s the US dollar steadily appreciated against the euro, and indeed against other reserve currencies (mainly the Japanese yen), so did the Argentinian peso.

Harsh Conundrum

Under the currency board arrangements, the growth of the money supply was constrained by net capital inflows and credit was rationed: small and medium sized enterprises had to pay rates that bordered on usury. As a consequence, the banking system continuously sought to expand its dollar assets on which its leverage depended to avoid the likelihood of a monetary crunch. This was the harsh conundrum: keeping convertibility on a par with the US dollar implied a rising debt or a credit squeeze since the economy was not sufficiently competitive at the fixed and steadily appreciating exchange rate.

On the side of public finances, theory demanded that the budget be balanced and practice required that the government keep a deficit as small as possible. As it has been mentioned, however, unassisted unemployment remained above 15 per cent. No democratic government can sustain such a high rate for long and certainly not one that still had a strong populist penchant, especially in outlying provinces where most of it was concentrated. In spite of appalling inefficiency, pressure rose for the public sector to offer the remedy by creating much needed compensating employment. In a country with a feeble tax base like Argentina, this meant rising peripheral governments' budget deficits that the federal one had to offset by transfers. A balanced budget became wishful thinking and its financing increasingly problematic. Given the traditional general public's distrust of government bonds, underwriters were to be found either within the financial sector or directly abroad. Banks bought government bonds but, given the currency board rationing of reserves, they had to sell them on the international market in exchange for dollar balances for which there was a high demand because of a high current account deficit. Buying dollar denominated public liabilities in exchange for pesos and then selling them abroad for actual dollar balances closed the gap, transforming private international debt into a public one making it expedient to place issuances directly abroad. Towards the end of the decade, government deficits increased as a consequence of a deep downturn and debt accordingly rose to unbearable heights. It is interesting to note that deficits and debt were a consequence of the deep imbalances engineered by the policies that had been undertaken since the inception of the Menem's administration and not their cause. All the symptoms of a pending financial crisis were then gathered: *(i)* an overvalued exchange rate, *(ii)* a structural current account deficit, *(iii)* a large external debt increasingly contracted on a short-term basis, *(iv)* a high public deficit.

What happened then followed a very classical pattern. Increasing borrowing requirements demanded the support of the International Monetary Fund, an institution that changed its attitude from praise to reprimand. Predictably, the root of external disequilibrium was seen in the excessive absorption originating from the government deficit and the onus of adjustment was accordingly placed on cutting public spending at a time, especially after 1998-1999, of a deepening recession. Compliance with this ill-advised measure brought about still lower activity levels, even more unemployment, falling tax receipts and, finally, larger fiscal deficits that required further external borrowing: the economy was thrown into a vicious circle. In 2000, Menem finally lost the general elections to an indecisive politician, Fernando De La Rua, who would not take the ultimate step of unhinging the currency from its dollar straitjacket, fearing an upper and middle class backlash that held dollar deposits and debt contracts (mostly mortgages). Menem left a poisoned legacy: on the strength of a political and public opinion blinded by international pressures and prominent economists' advice that entirely espoused the IMF belief in the orthodoxy of a balanced budget, a law was pushed through Congress mandating the government to legislate a zero budget deficit. De la Rua had his hands tied.

All the cards were laid out for a grand slam. In 2001, expectations ran high that the situation had become unbearable: foreign corporations who had replaced the state as a monopolist began to repatriate large peso balances, speculators and rich rentiers who had always kept their wealth placed abroad, i.e., the US financial market, stepped up capital flight. Dollar reserves were, accordingly, drained and reached an all time low much more rapidly than the money supply could be lowered to match whilst markets were no longer ready to buy any Argentinian liability. Capital flows were all outgoing and none incoming.

In December 2001, fears that devaluation would take place reached a feverish height and people from all walks of life began to withdraw their deposits to change them into dollars. But there were not enough dollars. As Christmas day neared, everybody sought to outpace his or her neighbour. On the morning on December 21, a run on the banks occurred. The government and monetary authorities had no choice: they had to let the currency float and declare all deposits unclaimable, for a temporary period, but long enough to cause incredible distress. Argentina has now painfully recovered, but it was left in a shambles amongst unprecedented misery and with a poverty line that rose to embrace more than 50 per cent of the population

Poland's Experience with Convertibility

In 1990, after a decade of disintegration I which, at its end, bordered on hyper-inflation, Poland's "planned economy" based on state ownership of the means of production was put to rest. An IMF-sponsored shock therapy brought about, within a short period, a market economy. Extensive, if at times chaotic, privatisation of firms and banks started. Private economic activities were legalised, prices freed, and shortages eliminated. Foreign trade was fully liberalised and tariff rates were drastically reduced. Following a dramatic devaluation, the exchange rate of the domestic currency, the zloty, was fixed and made internally convertible. The currency was convertible on almost all current account transactions. Importers had unrestricted access to foreign exchange. But capital account transactions were not liberalised. The restrictions practically prohibited official exports of capital. Then, the residents were obliged to repatriate and then sell their hard currency holdings to the state. The use of the Polish currency for invoicing and making payments in foreign trade was not allowed. The excessive fiscal squeeze and inordinately high interest rates imposed by the central bank, which were part and parcel of the initial stages of the shock therapy, had only a weak impact on inflation, which slowed down only sluggishly. By contrast, production and employment fell precipitously right away and then continued a downward drift for 30 months—cumulatively depressing real GDP by 20 per cent. In 1990, foreign trade played a positive role as the undervalued currency contributed to high trade and current account surpluses. But in 1991, as continuing inflation had finally resulted in high real overvaluation, large trade and current account deficits appeared.

1992-95

The new policy that was launched in 1992 responded with devaluation and very high tariffs and other protectionist measures (including selective subsidisation of exports). Then there was a change in the exchange rate regime, substituting a pre-announced sliding peg for the fixed one. Regular devaluation was linked to inflation so that real appreciation was effectively contained.

The illiberal policy initiated in 1992 proved spectacularly successful. It generated a sustained recovery over the years 1992-95, with an average annual GDP growth of 5 per cent. Fixed investment rose at. 10 per cent pa, inflation and unemployment kept falling, and public finances were broadly balanced. The trade and current accounts improved. A handsome surplus on the current account was generated in 1994, followed by a huge one in 1995. Thus, the economy pulled itself out of the "transitional recession" on its own—without incurring new foreign debt and without selling its assets to foreigners.

The real success of that period had much to do with the fact that Poland had not, until 1995, for various seasons, been a target for capital inflows. In the early 1990s, the intensity of international capital movements was, in general, quite low, partly on account of the recent crises (including the turbulent collapse of the first version of the European Monetary System). Moreover, the reputation of the former

Soviet bloc countries was very low at that time. Some of them (the former Yugoslav republics, the Baltic countries, the successor states of former Czechoslovakia) were still in the process of state-building. All of them were considered risky, unstable places facing an unknown future. Poland's reputation was particularly low because the country had defaulted on its huge public foreign debt (already in 1982). The restrictions on capital movements, though aimed primarily at preventing capital exports rather than imports, were not improving the country's standing. In these circumstances, the fact that nominal interest rates in Poland were still very high (inflation receding only gradually) did not—for several years—induce any significant capital inflows.

In the end, though, Poland fell victim to its own success. Actually, by 1994-95 Poland was the only "success case" among the former Soviet bloc countries. As such, it was becoming the darling of the international financial institutions (IMF, World Bank), western governments, and finally of the international business community, which eventually appreciated Poland's performance. Consequently, Poland was richly rewarded: first with generous treaties on the reduction and rescheduling of its foreign debt (1994), followed by the conclusion of the agreement on association with the European Union and admittance into the World Trade Organisation (WTO) and the Organisation for Economic Cooperation and Development (OECD). On its part, Poland accepted the obligations of Article VIII of the IMF statutes on full current account convertibility (June 1995). Besides, it pledged to dismantle, gradually, its trade protectionist scaffolding. This was soon followed by a whole series of further steps partially liberalising capital transactions: exporters were no longer obliged to convert their revenues into the domestic currency; residents (and domestic firms) were allowed to invest some (still limited) amounts in other OECD countries; domestic firms were permitted to engage in medium-term foreign exchange credit contracts with non-residents; the OECD set of regulations on foreign direct investment was adopted. Most importantly, already in 1995 the access to the short-term treasury bills market was opened to non-residents.

In 1995 Poland's official reserves rose abruptly, more than doubling, to over $ 14.5 billion. Only part of the increase in reserves was due to the high current ac-coi'.nt surplus. For the first time the country experienced high inflows of foreign direct investment, private portfolio capital and credits drawn by the private sector. Capital inflows were only natural, given the reduced levels of risks/uncertainty, the predictability of Poland's exchange rate (the pre-announced sliding peg) and the very high nominal levels of domestic interest rates (corresponding to inflation, running .at about 25 per cent in 1995). The sudden overabundance of foreign exchange did not bring down interest rates on credits denominated in domestic currency. Rather, these interest rates were actually increased as the National Bank of Poland (the central bank) attempted to sterilise the inflows by "mopping up" the excess liquidity accumulating in the commercial banking system. The sterilisation, which was quite costly, was only partially successful as it did not completely prevent a credit boom fuelling private consumption and investment. On the other hand, increased domestic interest rates induced even higher capital inflows. Very soon the National Bank saw no other way out but to allow the currency to float, within some bounds, around the "central parity", on the inter-bank forex market. Nominal appreciation followed immediately. Shortly afterwards the National Bank had to revalue the central parity even further. This alone produced huge gains to foreign speculators. The floating, which was to deter excessive short-term speculation by making it more risky, was outsmarted by the market, which quickly developed instruments allowing speculation all the same (first futures, then swaps and then more sophisticated currency and interest rate derivatives). The major players on the still rather shallow Polish forex financial markets were (and still are) the London-based traders gambling against Polish market participants (including the Treasury and the National Bank). It may be added that, as long as Polish interest rates were very high, the short-term speculation was not against the Polish currency. Such speculation was (and still is) potentially too costly. Under high interest rates speculation tends to inflate the value of the domestic currency—irrespective of its "fundamental value". Conversely, speculation may tend to force an excessive weakening of the currency if domestic interest rates are believed to be too low.

1996-2005

The policy changes, initiated in 1995 continued to unfold.

(1) Capital account liberalisation has continued. In 1997, non-residents were given access to treasury bonds. In 1998, residents were allowed to engage in some kinds of transactions in some categories of derivatives. Finally, in 2002, the Polish currency became almost fully convertible. The only remaining restrictions pertain to foreigners' acquisitions of farmland, and to some short-term transactions with non-OECD parties.

(2) There has been a steady evolution of the exchange rate regime. The devaluation factor for the "central parity" was progressively lowered, thereby increasingly losing touch with domestic inflation. In effect, monetary policy was losing control over real appreciation. At the same time, the bands around the "central parity" widened over time. The National Bank's involvement in the operation of the foreign exchange market was gradually reduced. This culminated in the pure free float formally introduced in early 2000. Actually, already in February 1998 the National Bank had burned its fingers during the attempts to stop currency speculation and withdrew from the forex market. The determination of the exchange rate has been left to the still shallow, and volatile, forex markets.

(3) Monetary policy has been increasingly relying on interest rate manipulations, formally aiming at controlling inflation only. This culminated in the adoption of inflation targeting already in 1998. But inflationary pressures calmed slowly all the same. Continuing capital inflows made it possible for the banks to expand lending even if that collided with

> the intentions of the National Bank. In effect,'domestic interest rates have been excessively high most of the time, leading to periodical high tides of foreign capital, "artificially" strengthening the currency. It may be added that the real interest rates on credit denominated in domestic currency had been very high (in excess of 10 per cent) from 1996 until 2004. (By contrast, real interest rates were very low, quite often close to being negative, until mid-1995). The problem monetary policy faced was (and essentially still is) that a rise in the interest rate meant to slow down credit growth was, at the same time, inducing higher inflows, which supported credit expansion. Conversely, cuts in interest rates meant to reduce capital inflows tend to strengthen credit expansion. Only occasionally, when major currency crises afflicted other "emerging markets" (as in mid-1996, in December 1997 and in September 1998) could monetary policy control domestic credit and inflation with a greater degree of efficiency. On such occasions, the domestic currency usually weakened, though never enough to eliminate the excessive real overvaluation that had accumulated since 1995.

The year 1995 was a turning point as far as the depth and scope of currency convertibility is concerned. At the same time, that year marked a change in monetary and exchange rate policies. Eclectic monetary policies, adjusting their goals to the varying requirements of the moment, were no longer possible. In particular, monetary policy had to abdicate its responsibility for stabilising the exchange rate. The change of policy paradigms has had definite and, on the whole, rather negative consequences.

First of all, strong real appreciation had immediate effects on foreign trade performance and the current account. Already in 1996 exports slowed down while imports expanded explosively. Within one year the trade surplus of 2.4 per cent of GDP turned into a deficit of 4.3 per cent. The current account surpluses of previous years were replaced by large deficits. Under continuing capital inflows and the resultant currency appreciation the current account deficits kept rising until early 2000 when they approached 9 per cent of the GDP. Interestingly, until 2001 (and also more recently) capital inflows overcompensated the current account deficits.

Secondly, the high GDP growth prior to 1995 was sustained only for a couple of years thereafter. But, as the contribution of foreign trade to growth became negative (already in 1996), growth was to be driven by consumption and (until 2000) by capital formation. However, unlike in the previous period, both consumption and capital formation were increasingly financed by rising foreign debt. That was one of the effects of the very high real domestic interest rates engineered by the National Bank. Poland's foreign debt (private and public combined) rose from 41 billion euro in 1995 to 75 billion euro in 2000. Currently it is close to 110 billion euros (of which private foreign debt is about 70 billion). The ballooning foreign debt is only one indication of the unsoundness of the course of development taken after 1995. Simultaneously, Poland has been selling off its assets. The bulk of the most efficient industrial firms, banks, insurance companies, utilities, etc., have already been sold to foreign multinationals, usually at huge discounts. Needless to say, without the "family silver" having been sold to foreigners. Poland's foreign debts would have been much higher.

Naturally, a loan-led and import-fed growth could not be sustained indefinitely. From 1998 growth was slowing down Several years of intensifying external competition (supported by the strong currency) and high real interest rates finally eroded the profits of the corporate sector and weakened the financial position of households and firms (snowballing debt). Unemployment, falling from 1994, rebounded. In 2000 the rate of unemployment reached 17 percent, rising to 20 per cent in the early 2000s. In 2001 GDP growth slowed down to a symbolic 1 per cent, followed by 1.4 per cent in 2002. The average GDP growth rate for the entire post-liberalisation period (1996-2005) is a lean 3.9 per cent, with gross fixed investment on average rising by about 4.2 per cent annually.

The stagnation of 2001-02 eventually made the job of

the National Bank easier. As the demand for credit dried up, the Bank risked, very reluctantly, cutting interest rates. A long overdue, if mild, currency depreciation followed. Nonetheless, the current (since 2003) recovery has been quite anaemic. Despite the recent relaxation of tight monetary policy, the exchange rate is still fundamentally too strong, and interest rates are too high. Wages have been suppressed for several years now. Consumption and domestic fixed investment have been rising only weakly. This seems to be a natural consequence of the exuberant debt-driven expansion of the late 1990s. Under suppressed domestic demand (and falling unit labour costs), there have been improvements in foreign trade. In the foreseeable future Poland may be condemned to an export-led growth-with rising shares of domestic income to be surrendered to the outside world in the form of interest and property income on foreign capital that has invaded the country since 1995. In 1995. 1.4 percent of the GDP was appropriated by the rest of the world. By 2004, foreigners' share in Poland's GDP rose to 4.6 percent.

Summing Up

There are two distinct periods in Poland's recent history, differing as far as the levels of external liberalisation are concerned. The first may be dated as 1992-95. The second started in 1995-96 and has not yet ended.

During the first period, imports were controlled through tariffs and other instruments, while exports were promoted through subsidies. Appreciation of the currency was controlled via a managed nominal exchange rate, which was possible under a rather illiberal approach to capital movements. Real interest rates were moderate. There was an acceleration of capital formation. The economy pulled itself out of a deep recession without incurring any new foreign debt -and without selling out its assets to foreigners.

During the second period, there has been a steady and rapid liberalisation of imports and a discontinuation of subsidisation of exports. More important!). capital inflows were liberalised all along—which paradoxically failed to bring down domestic interest rates. In fact, the high, essentially uninvited, capital inflows were responsible (via sterilisation operations) for the persistence of very high domestic interest rates. Moreover, under high capital inflows, there has been a tendency towards strong real appreciation. and this has impaired first exports and then overall growth):

In conventional/stories there is a "causality" running from high growth through high trade deficits to high compensatory capital inflows. Or, as it is often maintained, high-growth countries need "imports of foreign savings"—and this seems unimaginable without freedom of capital movements. Poland's experience does not support that story at all. In Poland's case the high growth in the illiberal years did not generate any need for "imports of foreign savings", or foreign capital. And, it turned out that foreign capital started to arrive in large quantities, upon being allowed to do so, precisely when it was not at all needed. Moreover, soon after arriving, the uninvited capital in fact impaired growth in the host country. The impairment took the form of undue currency appreciation, which in turn damaged the external competitiveness of the host country, producing high trade deficits. It was the influx of "foreign savings" which eventually crowded out, or suppressed, domestic savings. Only then, after impairing the host country's ability to generate high savings, may the inflow of foreign capital prove desirable, or even necessary. But, paradoxically, precisely then such capital may be reluctant to come. Or, it may just then show a propensity to extract high payments for the past "services".

Convertibility: Brazilian Experience

Macroeconomics in the Last 20 Years

Some would see Brazil as a country where macroeconomic policies swing between extremes. It is easy to identify periods since the second world war when the country wanted to integrate itself more fully with the international market, and other periods when there were calls for self-sufficiency and a need to strengthen state control over important sectors of the economy.

In the last 20 years, or so, the Brazilian economy can be clearly divided into three different phases. The first (1983-1994) was characterised by successive efforts to curb inflation, renegotiate external debt and reduce the current account deficit. In this period the country did not experience a large movement of capital, which would have limited the autonomy of economic policies, given that high inflation, capital controls and the default of 1987 had isolated the Brazilian economy from the international financial market.

The Real Plan, launched in July 1994, demarcates the beginning of the second phase (1994-1998), which drastically changed the previous perception. The limits imposed by the mobility of capital made clear the need for pro-market reforms to improve the "microeconomic fundamentals" that eventually would give sustainability to the reorientation of the economy and macroeconomic adjustment. Advocacy of liberalisation came for the most part from the academic mainstream, financial-market practitioners and a number of politicians. Some broad features of the Real Plan were: (i) it was established by a law; (ii) introduced some sort of fiscal adjustment; (iii) reduced price indexation; (iv) increased market deregulation and trade liberalisation; and (v) established a new currency (Real) with stable acquisitive power based upon an exchange rate anchor. Emphasis was placed on privatisation of public enterprises, incentives to private foreign investment, maintenance of freedom to movement of capital. The process of convertibility was enhanced, a trend that continues to currently take place.

The combination of financial liberalisation and a real interest rate differential between Brazil and the international capital market would have made possible a relatively fixed and overvalued exchange rate in order to allow a competitive shock and reduce the inertia! component of Brazilian inflation. The differential in interest rates also functioned to ensure a positive net inflow of external capital, to finance the balance of payments. The main criticism of this approach was its implicit external fragility: in the absence of a stable international environment there was a significant risk of speculative attack. Thus, the viability of the Real Plan depended basically on variables not controlled by policy-makers, such as the expectations of the financial market and the speed of regulatory procedures in Brazil's Congress. Moreover, international financial instability increased external vulnerability (due to the liberalisation of the capital account) through the so-called contagion effects, sudden drying up of capital inflows and speculative attacks on the exchange rate. In January 1999, these speculative attacks resulted in the collapse of the exchange rate regime. It is fair to say that the non-sustainability of the macro-economic model derived from what Obstfeld (1998) denominated as the "inconsistent trinity".

The third phase, which began in 1999 and continues today, was based on the adoption of an inflation target, a floating exchange rate regime and a generation of substantial primary surpluses. The aim of the fiscal policy was to reverse the unsustainable rising trend of the public debt/GDP ratio in 1994-98, despite the increasing tax burden. It is relevant to note that, as in the initial stages of the Real Plan, two important macro-economic functions were delegated to restrictive monetary policy: (i) to reduce inflation until it reached a "long-run steady state"; and (ii) to manage international capital flows in periods of financial stress. Another peculiar aspect that should be mentioned is that the operationalisation of the inflation target in Brazil requires a higher real interest rate than the one necessary to satisfy the international parity condition. As a consequence, international arbitrage tends to overvalue the domestic currency, reducing the profitability of investments meant for production for the external market.

Although the Brazilian government was adopting most of the policies suggested by the international financial market, in 2002 the country suffered a sudden drying up of capital inflows and a large increase in outflows, due to acres is of confidence related to domestic electoral uncertainty. This is not a surprising outcome but the standard consequence of currency convertibility: the partial loss of autonomy in the conduct of economic policies.

Indeed, in the past Brazil has faced managerial difficulties, chiefly due to external shocks that are transmitted to the real economy by abrupt fluctuations in the exchange rate, which, in turn, reflect the instability of international capital flows. The result has been a disappointing macro-economic volatility. The trajectory of the economic indicators leads to the conclusion that the process of economic liberalisation has produced a volatile and quasi-stagnating impact on output (and hence of employment) and an adverse shock to investment. From 1995 to 2005, the average increase in GDP per capita was 1.15 per cent and the investment ratio as a proposition of GDP (removing the variation stocks) averaged 14.71 per cent.

Trends in Capital Account Legislation

Despite the financial crises in Mexico (1995), east Asia (1997) and Russia (1998), the general trend in Brazil since the late 1980s has been in the direction of greater financial openness. In 1987 the first liberal measures were introduced, when foreign investment companies and funds were allowed to operate in the country, and some portfolio investments were allowed. Another important point was the opening up of the securities market to foreign institutional investors in 1991. The "floating exchange rate market", introduced in 1988, allowed further liberalisation of residents' outflows, and the main change was the possibility of conversion from domestic to foreign currency through non-resident accounts. In practice, residents in Brazil could deposit funds in a non-resident account held in a domestic bank, which could convert domestic to foreign currency. Such accounts represented the introduction of de facto convertibility.

Other measures which enhanced convertibility and stimulated foreign capital flows during the 1990s were a general tax reduction on remittances abroad, the authorisation to issue external debt instruments denominated in foreign currency and the permission to foreign investors to operate in the options and futures markets. Furthermore, the issuance abroad of convertible debentures was authorised and so too the depository receipts representing Brazilian securities.

Notwithstanding the liberal trend, from 1993 to 1996

new capital controls were adopted which were motivated by concerns regarding the cost of sterilising capital inflows. The restrictive actions involved quantitative controls and price-based measures through the use of the financial transactions tax. Looking at the way these controls were implemented leads to the conclusion that when there was a substantial increase in capital inflows, policy- makers placed limitations on inflows and stimulated outflows. The measures easing outflows made it clear that the overall objective was to reduce net inflows without affecting the liberal project of increasing integration with the international financial market.

Since the first half of the 2000s, nonresidents have been allowed to invest in the same instruments in the financial and capital markets as residents. The current registration process of external flows by the central bank of Brazil has become a documentary requirement instead at an active authorisation process. Regardless of the large liberalisation, the present convertibility of the Real is based on an apparatus of rules of different kinds made in different circumstances, instead of a previously announced, organised and gradually implemented legal process. The consequence is an excessively bureaucratic and complicated system that obstructs the attainment of the "advantages" of financial liberalisation.

The truth about capital account opening in Brazil is that the economic rationale behind it was to make possible the "major macroeconomic objective" of price stabilisation based on an exchange rate anchor. Thus, the procedural order did not follow the sequence and timing prescribed in the literature. The result was a vast openness without the necessary improvements and maturity in the related institutions or macroeconomic indicators.

Hopes and Fears

Two undesired collateral effects of the Real Plan, both relating to capital account convertibility, were: (i) deterioration of the external sector; and (ii) precarious public finances. With regard to the external sector, the overvalued exchange rate-based stabilisation programme led to large current account deficits. Notwithstanding the non-sustainability of the consequent increase in external debt and the level of the overvalued exchange rate, the financial market supported the programme (mainly by portfolio inflows) from July 1994 to the end of 1998. In addition, the controlled exchange rate associated with the interest rate differ debt by the private sector. In January 1999, capital outflows forced a drastic policy shift in order to avoid a complete depletion of government foreign reserves.

The exchange rate depreciation, related to the adoption of a floating exchange system and to the crisis of confidence in 2002, stimulated a reorientation of production in direction of tradeable goods, resulting in expanding trade balance surpluses. The floating regime also provides further incentives for borrowers to better assess exchange risks. The uncertainty that this regime introduces makes it highly risky to issue foreign currency debt, in particular for agents who do not have dollar revenues (the non-tradeable sector). These incentives and newer export stimuli resulted in an improvement of the external indicators, as the external debt/ GDP ratio dropped from 3.6 in January 1999 to 0.8 in March 2006. Thus, Brazil experienced what the literature had already pointed out in the early 1990s: the app private exchange rate regime for a financially open economy is the one capable of absorbing part of the external shocks through flexible relative prices.

The Real Plan required an initial fiscal adjustment that should have been further expanded, but this adjustment has been postponed. Actually, despite some advances in this area, in the last 10 years fiscal policy has been marked by a continuous increase in the tax burden. Since 1994 the tax burden expanded from about 26 per cent of GDP to around 40 per cent of GDP today. Government expend, increased faster than GDP, with the opposite occurring in government capital investment outlays, currently at negligible levels. What is the relationship between these "residues of Real Plan" and account convertibility?

The defenders of free capital movement frequently mention that one of its advantages would be the constant supervision of economic policies by the financial market direction of "prudent and/or responsible" policies. The Brazilian case shows precisely wisely the opposite: inflows have not been concerned about fiscal and exchange "irresponsibility" and have eagerly responded to arbitrage opportunities until "market mood" suddenly changes, resulting in a mix of herd behaviour and I speculative attack on the national currency. In reality, the inflows supported a deterioration of the external account and helped delay the indispensable fiscal adjustment. The Brazilian experience corroborates the interpretation that the international financial market seems to impose a sudden and pungent discipline through a financial crisis, and not a constant and soft adjustment of the required policies.

Another aspect indicated in the literature as one of the benefits of financial opening is the "efficiency effect" attributable to the intensification in competition and the adoption of more sophisticated financial techniques. Some new technologies were introduced in the Brazilian financial sector and the firms were efficient in the sense of selecting the best profit opportunity that the market offered. Nonetheless, the indicators of financial density in Brazil remain lower than international levels, revealing a paradox of competitiveness/efficiency on the one side and low macroeconomic functionality on the other. Moreover, the credit facilities that exist for consumers and firms, besides being limited, have high spreads. The averages of two indicators illustrate these arguments. From January 1999 to February 2006, the total credit/GDP ratio was 27.31 per cent and the annual spread in credit operations 41.96 per cent (which refers to the difference between the cost of borrowing funds and the interest rate earned).

The high interest rate differential necessary to maintain capital inflows resulted in a high opportunity cost of credit for productive investment, since public bonds carried less risk, greater return and were more liquid than private sector debt instruments. This perverse relation »transferred income from consumers and entrepreneurs to the public sector and rentiers, redirected part of the credit that could have been channeled to the private sector and put greater pressure on the real interest rate, harming further the prospects of future growth.

Defenders of financial opening also affirm that foreign investors have a high aversion to corruption, which could enhance the quality of public administration. This statement is without solid proof in Brazil. In 2005, for example, the country witnessed one of the biggest revelations of corruption in high places. However, since the allegations did not reach the citadels of orthodox economic policy and because the main explanatory variable of capital movement (the interest rate) was very high in relation to international levels, these allegations did not result in sudden capital outflows. On the contrary, the real effective exchange rate registered a strong appreciation of 15.8 per cent, the country risk (EMBI+ Brazil) fell 28.8 per cent and the Sao Paulo stock market index registered an increase of 27.7 percent led by overseas investments. Therefore, the macroeconomic benefits of capital account convertibility are questionable. It is possible that Brazil has already suffered greatly from the costs of hasty financial liberalisation.

A Recent Problem

In an environment of capital account convertibility, central banks of countries with weak currencies have difficulties in simultaneously maintaining credit and money stability. The reason is the existence of a hierarchy between currencies, defining distinct conditions in the organisation and operation of the financial and exchange markets. Moreover, the volatility of monetary conditions along with the presence of fragile institutions, inadequately developed markets and an instability in risk aversion (illusions and peculiarities) have an effect on the variation in investment. This being the circumstance, it is crucial to manage liquidity in strong currencies, as well as accumulate international reserves and current account surpluses, with the purpose of preventing external shocks that may disturb the autonomy (even in relative terms) of the main domestic monetary variables (interest and exchange rates).

It is not only in periods of risk aversion that financial

opening has an adverse effect on economic variables. Actually, in periods of voluminous international liquidity, the national currency tends to appreciate, especially where interest rate differentials are significant. This is one of the most recent and unfavourable problems faced by the Brazilian economy. The graph shows the inverse relationship between the real interest rate less the sovereign risk premium (EMBI+ Brazil) and the real effective exchange rate. The period coincides with the last monetary restriction that was necessary to reach the established inflation target. It is important to say that although the appreciation took place, the Central Bank of Brazil in the same period bought $ 32 billion in international reserves, doubling its level and showing that "the dirty float" is not sufficient to avoid currency appreciation when international capital flows can freely move in and out of the country.

The virtuous trajectory of the trade balance after adoption of the floating exchange regime, expanded the supply of foreign currency, raised confidence in some indicators of external vulnerability and reduced the country's risk premium. All these factors influence the demand for assets denominated in domestic currency, which acts in the direction of appreciation. Nonetheless, the monetary policy is a determinant of the exchange rate direction, since it defines the conditions of international arbitrage.

The actual level of the exchange rate is lower than the average in the period of controlled exchange rate (1994-98), which history shows was an unsustainable value. This overvaluation has consequences regarding the capability and incentives for new investments, especially in sectors more sensitive to variations in profitability. In fact, since September 2004, the 12-month accumulated growth rate of manufactured exports registered a significant fall (from around 24 per cent in the last quarter of 2004 to roughly 6 per cent in March 2006). At the same time, the export profitability index declined, reaching its lowest level of the last 12 years in March 2006.

Furthermore, the overvaluation of the Brazilian economy reduces the number of sectors capable of profitable export returns. In this vein, this tends to concentrate the growth of exports in sectors that had the "compensation effect" of an increase in international prices, or in sectors that had a considerable comparative advantage. Recent indicators of export performance show an increasing concentration in agricultural commodities.

Concluding Remarks

The Brazilian experience with capital account convertibility and the enforced conventional measures to protect the financial system seem to be more dangerous to the country's social-economic progress than what the supporters of such a strategy may suppose. A standard conclusion of the mainstream literature in this matter indicates that the faster countries privatise and liberalise, the better. Our analysis suggests that, contrary to such a view, the speed of capital account convertibility is negatively associated with sustained growth, stability and a more equitable income distribution. On the contrary, it confirms that strong institutions are very important for avoiding extreme measures. The Brazilian experience definitely shows that the excessive volatility of the real effective exchange rate and the high real interest rates reveal a non-synergetic environment. In conclusion, more careful management policies are indispensable to circumvent severe financial crises associated with imprudent capital account convertibility.

5

Impact of Convertibility in Semi-industrialised Economies

In this essay, we analyse capital account opening, which was part of a sequence of trade and financial sector reforms that Mexico undertook during the 1980s and 1990s, when a new generation of politicians and public servants came to power. After its first steps, Mexico hastened capital account opening, because of the worsening of the current account that resulted from trade liberalisation and commercial banking deregulation policies. We argue that such a development strategy did not contribute to an acceleration of income growth and stabilisation of the balance of payments, but hindered economic expansion. It ignored two important features of developing countries, which are their dependence on foreign technology and the weakness of their national currencies.

We organise the paper in six sections. The first describes capital account rules before the 1982 debt crisis, and the breakdown of the institutional setting because of negotiations for debt-restructure under the Brady Plan. In sections II and III, we show the disruptive effects the country's opening to unmanageable international capital flows had on the real and financial domestic markets, which eventually steered the economy to the twin crises of 1994. In sections IV and V, we consider the role C growing foreign control of domestic further in disintegration of domestic production worsening of the current account, and increasing external financial dependency after the crisis. We also call attention to the implications of the country's dependence on foreign technology and the weakness of its currency. In section VI we summarise our conclusions.

I. Financial Liberalisation under Washington Consensus

Mexico's economic policies were earlier based in the so-called import substitution strategy and came in unison with strong state intervention. Thus, they were similar to the policies adopted in the other large Latin American countries, except for the following. From the time when Mexico replaced its metallic currency by a public fiduciary currency, in the 1930s, free convertibility has been a main objective of economic policy. A lengthy border (more than 3,000 km) with the United States, and the US monetary authorities support for stabilisation of the peso-dollar exchange rate have since then dissuaded Mexican governments from instituting exchange rate controls' [Cardero 1984].

Therefore, controls on the capital account of the balance of payments were always mild. Their aim was to foster economic development, by protecting-^ domestic producers from foreign competitors and preventing speculation on domestic assets. Stabilising the exchange rate was not their main purpose.

The 1982 currency crisis, and the debt negotiations under the Brady Plan that followed came with the arrival of a new generation of politicians and public servants. Though they belonged to the political party which had traditionally ruled the country, they were much more attuned to neoliberal ideas. In this new context, the government decided to remove prevailing restrictions on foreign investment, and to carry out often liberalising reforms under the Washington Consensus guidelines.

The proponents of this development strategy relied on the efficient market hypothesis. They claimed that trade liberalisation, financial market deregulation and free international capital mobility would bring about many kinds of benefits to indebted developing countries. First, they would pull fresh foreign resources into these economies, which would contribute to modernising their productive structure. Second, they would enable domestic producers to compete more favourably in the most dynamic segments of International markets. Producers would be able to import the high technology inputs not yet produced domestically, and reduce costs by importing cheaper inputs from abroad. Third, they would benefit consumers and stimulate a more efficient use of productive resources by exposing domestic producers to foreign competition. Fourth, they would increase domestic savings and improve the quality of investment, by removing interest rate ceilings and abolishing bank credit rules. Finally, these reforms would compel governments to set up good policies and improve their performance, to avoid free markets imposing their discipline [Eatwell arid Taylor 2000; Cardero 2000].

From 1983 to 1987, the authorities hastily opened the domestic market to foreign trade. They reduced import and tariffs dramatically, and they removed non-tariff restrictions. At the same time they promoted bonded export manufacturing companies. In this period, capital account liberalisation began, and the government approved up to 100 per cent of foreign ownership in firms in non-oil export industries. Non-oil exports grew at an average annual rate of 18 per cent in that period, stimulated by currency undervaluation and depressed wage rates. Also, the share of firms with majority foreign capital ownership in export sales rose from 22 per cent in 1983 to 53 percent in 1987. In the commercial banking sector, direct credit controls and interest rate regulation were also abolished. By the end of the 1980s, once the financial institutions had become solvent again the government began their denationalisation. By 1990, the denationalisation process was complete. In 1989. When negotiations for restructuring the external debt ended, the government began to speed up capital account liberalisation.

It reduced limits to corporate foreign ownership in activities that accounted for nearly 75 per cent of GDP. It also allowed foreign investors to buy domestic securities and public enterprises put on sale, and to carry out swap operations with domestic indebted firms, as proposed in the Brady Plan.

Besides, the authorities allowed domestic financial institutions to operate in international financial markets; with some minor limits they let banks borrow abroad. They also allowed non-financial firms to place securities in foreign stock markets. Finally, the government gained cooperation agreements with foreign monetary authorities, stock exchanges and multilateral organisations, with the aim of helping to open the capital market [Cardero 2000; Guillen 2000].

In 1993, foreign financial institutions got permission to operate and place foreign securities in the domestic stock market. Shortly thereafter, the Mexican government subscribed to the North America Free Trade Agreement (NAFTA). NAFTA called for investors from other member countries to have the freedom to repatriate dividends and interest, enjoying equal treatment with national investors. At the same time it protected every foreign investment from adverse policy measures that member country governments could impose in the future.

In 1995 Mexico joined the OECD, and though the Multilateral Investment Agreement was not negotiated, a few years later the country signed a bilateral free trade agreement with the European Community, which included the core clauses of the MIA proposal as well as the provisions already incorporated in NAFTA on foreign investment, international payments and intellectual property. That agreement came into force in 2000.

II. Short-Term Capital Inflow, Stock Market Inflation and the Private Credit Boom

Capital market opening pulled to the country huge international financial resources. From 1989 to 1994, Mexico received $101,935 million, because of three particular circumstances abroad. First, the US had an economic recession in the early 1990s. Second, the regulations of the US Securities Exchange Commission were changed. Third, international interest rates started to fall [Ros and Lustig 1999].

The huge inflow of foreign capital had four destabilising effects in the economy. First, it appreciated the exchange rate, and it widened the current account deficit. Second, it encouraged commercial bank lending to the private sector, even as their share of lending to the government declined. Third, it induced banks to increase their exposure in foreign currency, given that domestic lending rates were nearly five times higher than inter bank lending rates in Eurodollar markets. Finally, it inflated the domestic stock market, which was too thin and shallow to absorb the enlarged demand for securities from foreign institutional investors at stable prices.

Despite the growing trade imbalance, the country piled up foreign reserves at a rapid pace. The government could therefore maintain the exchange rate peg. As inflation fell, international reserves increased, and the government showed concern for maintaining a stable nominal exchange rate, mainly through high domestic interest rates. Foreign investors' confidence too increased; and because of the short-term capital gains that foreign investors could fetch thanks to rising stock prices, capital inflows were further stimulated.

Financial market deregulation, and commercial bank denationalisation, hindered central bank efforts to sterilise such sizeable capital inflows. Open market operations were of little help in regulating domestic liquidity, because interest rate differentials were too large; and as they raised interest rates, they had the perverse effect of further increasing capital inflows.

From 1989 to 1994, domestic banking credit climbed from 27 to 52 per cent of GDP; and credit to the private sector rose from 14 to 38 per cent of GDP in the same period. During the process, the rate of domestic private savings fell from 17 to 11 per cent of GDP between 1988 and 1994. Since the government budget was roughly in balance, some authors assign a key role for that fall to the rise in consumer credit (see for example Ros and Lustig 1999). We do not share this outlook and we propose that the fall in the domestic saving rate was the result of financial liberalisation. We can argue our point with aid of the macroeconomic accounting equation for saving in an open economy:

$S\Delta + SS = SH = P — Sf$ where SP is private savings, SΔ is government savings, SH is domestic savings, IP is private investment, and Sf is foreign savings (equal to, under simplification, to the current account deficit).

We have already mentioned that in Mexico's experience, financial liberalisation contributed to appreciation of the domestic currency. This, coupled with trade liberalisation, brought about a huge rise in the trade and current account deficits. As a result, the relative share of domestic savings in the GDP markedly fell, even as the relative share of investment in GDP rose; and in fact rose at a faster rate than private consumption. Specifically, from 1992 to 1994, the trade deficit averaged 4 per cent of GDP, and it reached almost 7 per cent of GDP in 1994, even as the economy was growing at the moderate rate of 4 per cent a year.

Foreign direct investment had negligible effects on income growth in the first half of the 1990s, because most of it involved takeovers of existing firms [Guillen 2000]. Stock market inflation too did not have a significant influence on the rate of capital accumulation, since net investment was mostly financed out of retained earnings.

III. Reversal of Portfolio Foreign Investments and the 1994-95 Twin Crises

Despite the steady growth of the current account deficit, multilateral financial institutions, Mexican policy-makers, and many economic analysts in the private sector kept on praising Mexico's liberalising strategy. They based their optimism on achievements such as the following. First, a falling rate of inflation (from 30 per cent in 1990 to 7 per cent in 1994). Second, the success achieved in fiscal consolidation (with nearly three years of government surpluses). Third, the boost in manufactured exports, which had been expanding at a phenomenal annual average rate. However, they overlooked other disturbing indicators. One was the strong growth of imports (at an annual average rate of growth of 20 per cent from 1989 to 1994). Another was the currency mismatch in banks' assets and liabilities. Last but not the least, they did not consider the growing share of bad loans in bank's portfolios.

We may illustrate the state of confusion about the Mexican economy's prospects with the following statement made by the governor of Mexico's central bank, just two weeks before the exchange rate crisis of December 1994 broke out: "The size of the current account deficit is, in a way, a measure of the country's success, not of its failure... The greater the success of Mexico as an attractive country for investment, the bigger the current account deficit will be".

The change in US monetary policy beginning in 1994, which launched an upward trend in international interest rates, brought about a sudden decline in the flow of foreign capital to Mexico and other developing economies. First, domestic banks faced difficulties in sustaining their credit lines in foreign banks. Second, non-financial enterprises were unable to roll over their foreign loans. Finally, the government was compelled to exchange dollar denominated securities for the peso denominated bonds which until then were held by foreign institutional investors and to shorten the terms to maturity.

Some of the country's main economic indicators remained stable. However, a speculative attack against the currency developed. The latter took place owing to'political events, and because of the suspicion that under prevailing conditions in international financial markets, domestic economic agents would be unable to discharge their external obligations, Over 1994, the country's foreign reserves declined from $24 billion to $6 billion. In December 1994, given the high degree of financial fragility, the self-fulfilling prophecies of domestic and foreign investors plunged the country into an exchange rate crisis. This straightaway led to a financial crisis, because of the high level of domestic banks' exposition in foreign currency.

The central bank imposed a tight monetary policy on the economy in order to reduce the inflationary effects of currency devaluation and to put a brake on the substitution of foreign currency denominated assets for domestic financial assets. But naturally the credit crunch made matters worse.

High interest rates and stiff credit conditions, as well as a reduced import capacity pushed the economy into a deep recession, which led to a fall in GDP by about 6 per cent in 1995. The fall in income and profits, jointly with the rise in interest rates, rapidly eroded the quality of banks' credit assets and the guarantees given as collateral. As the share of bad performing loans in banks portfolio rose, a credit crunch developed.

Under such conditions, which are characteristic of countries with a weak currency that liberalise the capital account of the balance of payments, the central bank was unable to fulfill its function of a lender ,if last resort. Since the economic authorities were unwilling to introduce controls which were needed to cope with an external financial crisis, foreign capital appeared as the only possible source of liquidity. In the first stage, this relief came from an emergency financial package negotiated with multilateral financial institutions and the US government, under severe conditionality. To gain international official assistance, the government compromised and agreed to carry out policies friendly to foreign investment. Also, the collapse in domestic firms' market values, jointly with the exchange rate depreciation, made possible the return of foreign private capital flows to the country. But now foreign investors had more favourable conditions.

In the succeeding years, the country has gradually recovered from the 1994 crisis. However, the distortion caused by the growing participation of foreign capital in strategic sectors of the economy has dramatically changed its structure and institutions. In a certain sense these changes overhauled the economic (as well as political) fundamentals of Mexico's economy and society.

IV. Resurgence of FDI and Worsening of Current Account

The 1994 financial crisis hastened opening of financial services to foreign direct investment. In NAFTA negotiations, domestic firms in these activities had received favourable treatment, since the treaty protected them from foreign competition for six years. During this period foreign intermediaries could only have 15 per cent of the domestic market. One policy objective had been to strengthen domestic industrial and financial conglomerates, to develop scale and scope economies that would enable them to compete more advantageously in international markets.

The exchange rate crisis killed these ambitions. The 1994-95 crisis forced the government to bail out the banking sector. Three years later, as a means to recapitalise those institutions, the government resigned from the NAFTA safeguard. It passed a law that enabled foreign investors to hold up to 100 per cent of domes tic banks equity, without limiting their share in the local market. The market share of foreign capital controlled banks increased from 1 per cent in 1994, to 40 per cent in 1999, 53 per cent in 2000, and 90 per cent in 2004 [Macedo 2000; Correa and Maya 2002; Berumen 2004]. That share is the highest among OECD countries.

Without the support of their banks and under the pressure of foreign competition, the larger conglomerates developed new strategies for survival, which entailed investments abroad and associations with foreign producers. For smaller firms, the joint effect of the domestic credit crunch and imports competition was devastating.

By contrast, trade liberalisation and opening of the capital account pulled towards the country foreign direct investors. The latter took advantage of lower labour and transport costs, and relocalised some production processes to compete more favourably in the US market [Moreno Brid et al 2005]. The in-bond industries also flourished.

As the economy became more export-oriented, it also showed decreasing domestic integration. The income elasticity of imports, which hovered between 0.6 and 1.8 before trade liberalisation, jumped to 3 in the period 1983-2003 (Moreno-

Brid 1999). Now, the exporting firms are also the largest importers (for example imports by in-bond industries account for 80 per cent of their output value).

The Mexican experience confirms that trade liberalisation with an open capital account, in countries dependent on foreign technology, brings about a widening current account deficit, which makes the country increasingly dependent on foreign capital inflows.

Foreign direct investment, which is usually considered superior to external debt, has negatively affected the economy because of several reasons. The most important reason is that a large part of foreign direct investment involved takeover of existing local firms, and another large share was deployed in exporting industries with high import requirements. Formally, these are manufacturing firms turning out sophisticated goods. But they are little more than assembly plants of multinationals. Besides, owing to the lack of an industrial strategy, investment (domestic or foreign) was not encouraged in the input industries, and the elasticity of imports rose exponentially. Therefore, a large part of the demand induced by exports leaked abroad, the foreign trade barrier to growth [Thirlwall 1979] was not lifted, and the growth rate of output remained modest. Thus, while Mexico's share in world manufacturing exports rose about 2.2 percentage points between 1980 and 1997, its share in world manufacturing value added declined about 0.7 percentage points.

Another reason foreign direct investment has failed to bring about the expected results is because of the high market power of foreign firms. Since these firms tend to be large and powerful, the degree of competition in the branches of activity in which they engage has declined. In addition, foreign investment also has promoted foreign indebtedness, because takeovers are usually leveraged and foreign firms also rely on finance provided by their main companies. Finally, the assumed benefit of a fixed investment vis-a-vis more volatile short-term flows, such as loans or portfolio investments, becomes much undermined when shares of foreign firms are traded in the local stock exchange and changes in ownership can rapidly occur [Vidal 2001].

All in all, trade liberalisation with opening of the capital account, in a semi-industrialised economy dependent on foreign technology, holds back domestic industrial integration and produces a more binding balance of payments constraint to growth. This pattern of development has posed a dilemma to Mexican policy-makers. As the current account worsens and larger capital inflows are required, they are compelled to preserve nominal exchange rate stability. Now though this policy, successfully lowers inflation, it also brings about a further worsening of the trade account.

V. Financial Intermediation by Foreign Banks and Changing Ownership Structure

Local firms' direct investments abroad, much like foreign direct investment inflows, are always leveraged operations, and they entail issuing liabilities denominated in foreign currency. In 2002, Mexican investments abroad amounted to $ 65 billion, from which $ 45 billion was deposits and credits. In the same year, foreign investment in Mexico exceeded 50 per cent of GDP: direct investments accounted for 20 per cent of GDP, and portfolio investments plus credit loans represented 30 per cent [Garrido 2005].

We note an increasing share of foreign financing from 1995 onwards in the largest domestic firms. These liabilities show longer terms to maturity compared with local currency loans, but they entail interest and currency risks, which endanger capital control by Mexican stockholders in the future. This is so, because in global competition, multinational enterprises are backed by their banks that provide them with credit in hard currency, and thus have both technological and financial superiority [Garrido 2005; Vidal 2000]. These conditions expose even the largest domestic firms to hostile takeovers by foreign financial groups [Singh and Weisse 1998].

Domestic banks under foreign control have gradually reduced credit to domestic production units. Instead, they have increasingly engaged in government securities trading as well as in more sophisticated operations with financial derivatives; and they direct the lower credit flows mostly to consumer loans and mortgages.

In the future, however, things may change. By law, banks are in charge of private pension funds administration and new rules enable them to invest up to 20 per cent of workers' savings in foreign securities. Therefore, it is likely that they will provide support to foreign firms as a substitute for domestic producers. This provision will, in all likelihood, strengthen the financial superiority of foreign firms vis-a-vis their domestic competitors.

VI. Closing Remarks

Our analysis shows that the optimistic expectations about the effects of capital account liberalisation have not taken place in the Mexican economy. In opposition, reforms liberalising foreign investment have exposed the economy to the instability of international financial markets, and have produced at least the following negative outcomes: (i) Currency overvaluation and current account worsening, (ii) Enlarged capital market price volatility and financial speculation, (iii) A decline in private domestic savings, (iv) Financial fragility in the banking sector, and eventually the need to sell the banks to foreign institutions, (v) A rapid increase in foreign ownership of exporting firms, disintegration of the domestic industrial structure, bankruptcy of thousands of small size firms, and the rise in income elasticity of imports, (vi) A growing share of external finance in leading domestic firms, and the associated risk of future increases in foreign ownership, (vii) A decline in the rate of income growth, as the more severe balance of payments constraint sets a lower limit on domestic market expansion.

A Practitioner's Perspective

This essay attempts to examine the issue of capital account convertibility (CAC) from a practitioner's perspective. Unlike some other domains of economic policy, there is perhaps more convergence between policy-makers and practitioners on the issue of free mobility of capital. Memories of the Asian crisis in 1997 still linger and the crisis-hit economies were known to have regimes of substantial capital mobility. New risks have emerged on the back of a global liquidity surplus that has enhanced the appetite for risk and led to substantial enhancement of leveraged "carry trades" into markets. These could reverse if the global liquidity cycle turns. The ultimate victims of macroeconomic shocks are "micro" entities—banks, corporations and individuals. Both practitioners and policy-makers are equally interested in insulating them from the potential risks that the unbridled transfer of capital across borders can entail. Hence, practitioners -at least the majority of them in India -would rather that the government continue with its measured changes in the degree of capital mobility than go in for "full" capital convertibility in haste.

However, there is a consensus within the practitioner community that the government could take advantage of the continuous improvement in economic conditions to open up some more sluices for the flow of capital. Simultaneously, the kinks and anomalies within the current regime of convertibility (which work effectively as capital controls) need to be ironed out. Some of these may not technically fall in the traditional CAC domain. However, since they impede the free flow of capital, it is useful to review them. These initiatives are not exclusively in the central bank's domain but need coordinated action by the central bank, the finance ministry and other agencies of government.

Reviewing CAC

One critical aspect of CAC in the Indian context needs to be clarified right at the outset. The general perception that CAC is essentially about allowing larger outflows of capital is incorrect. The move towards capital convertibility is as much about removing the barriers to inflows as much as it is about allowing greater outflows. This is important since it relates the need for CAC to imperatives of funding India's growth. It also means that the central bank must rethink its entire paradigm of currency and interest rate management.

For instance, if capital inflows indeed pick up, the central bank might want to reconsider its policy of sterilised intervention that it follows in the currency and money markets. The costs of sterilisation are well known and it is also established that sterilisation often works to attract higher capital flows, pushing the monetary system into a spiral.

It might be useful, at this stage, to do a quick review of some of the improvements in the fundamentals on which the case for CAC is based. A number of the preconditions for convertibility that the Tarapore Committee (II) of 1997 (Tarapore-I as it is commonly referred to) had specified, have either been met or are close to being met. Importantly, the "soundness" indicators for external balances are significantly better than the thresholds set by Tarapore-I. Foreign exchange reserves, for instance, cover about 13 months of imports—the committee had asked for a minimum of six months. The Tarapore Committee had specified a maximum ratio of external debt servicing to current receipts of 20 per cent—the ratio currently stands at 7 per cent. The improvement in domestic fundamentals is less dramatic, but nonetheless encouraging.

Most practitioners would argue that these highly aggregated "top-down" indicators do not fully reflect the improvement in more "microeconomic" spheres in India. Indian companies, for one, have seen significant improvement in productivity and governance standards. There has been considerable consolidation in industry and a number of Indian companies operate at global scales. The quantum jump in the activity and output of the knowledge-based industries, such as information technology has helped the process of integration of the Indian economy with the external world.

From a capital account perspective, these changes have translated into an increase in foreign investor interest in Indian industry. This has been in the form of direct investment and portfolio investment. The average inflow of portfolio and foreign direct investment in the period 2004-05 to 2006-07 is likely to be $ 13.25 billion compared to an average of $ 5.7 billion in the five preceding years. This shift in investment trajectory appears to be sustainable going forward.

Diversification of Inflows

There is also a visible diversification of the source of these capital flows. The pattern of foreign institutional investor (FIT) inflows into Indian equity markets is a good example. Foreign investments into the Indian equity markets have historically been dominated by the US and Europe. However, over the last three years, Japan, South Korea and west Asia have emerged as significant investors in Indian equity. Informal estimates put the flows from far eastern economies into the Indian equity markets at $3 billion in 2005 and the first quarter of 2006.

How can greater CAC match this appetite for Indian paper with the needs of local companies, financial institutions and individuals? It might be prudent to start with the case for liberalising flows into and out of the domestic banking system. Banks are permitted to raise only 25 per cent of their tier-I capital within their open position and maturity mismatch limits. They are not allowed to raise external commercial borrowings (ECBs) either or sell securitised paper in the international market. Their investment in overseas money markets is limited to $ 10 million and $ 25 million in debt paper.

This gives rise to a number of problems. First, the absence of freer short-term flows from and into the banking system works against aligning Indian interest rates with global rates. This effectively leads to large arbitrage opportunities that have to be tackled with another set of barriers and controls. It also abets the development of semi-official markets like the non-deliverable forwards (NDF) market which is seen to reflect more "realistic" implicit interest rates. While the Indian central bank has no control over the NDF market, critical asset markets like foreign currency market have started to take cues from the NDF rather than the local forward market. This is certainly an unhealthy trend.

The curb on ECBs starves banks of long-term funds and the effect spills over to the real sector. This could be a binding constraint when the economy is going through an investment upsurge. While larger companies can circumvent the domestic banking system and access foreign loans directly, small and medium scale enterprises (that are perfectly creditworthy) often do not have direct access to global markets and have to turn to local banks.

Again, while the domestic market for securitised debt (non-distressed loans), the appetite for this paper remains confined really to short tenor debt. However, there is a growing supply of longer tenor paper in categories such as mortgage and car loans. Access to international markets would go a long way in developing the market for securitised assets at the medium and long ends of the tenor spectrum. In short, there appears to be a strong case for allowing banks to borrow more both for short term and the long term.

There are certainly legitimate concerns about "weak banks" being exposed to additional risks that access to foreign markets engender. This strengthens the case for greater consolidation of Indian banks in the long term. An interim solution is to introduce a liberal cap on borrowings for the banking system as a whole and then ask banks to approach the RBI for individual limits on the basis of the strength of their balance sheet. This would automatically weed out the weaker banks. The central bank is also likely to have concerns about the end-use of the funds borrowed abroad. As far as these are concerned, the combination of prudential norms for bank exposures to different sectors and restrictions on end-use of external borrowings should guard against possible "misuse".

Differential Limits

Greater short-term debt on banks' books might potentially breed more volatility in interest and exchange rates. Thus, the RBI might want to raise the limits on banks in a more phased, measured manner than the limit on, say, ECBs. However, greater volatility is perhaps desirable to a degree and will encourage prudent practices such as "hedging" in the exchange market by Indian companies. Differential limits for different banks based on their balance sheet strength would mean that those best equipped to handle volatility are exposed to it. One must recognise that equity flows are perhaps more volatile than short-term debt and the monetary and financial system has learnt to live with the absence of any curbs on these flows. If greater volatility (stemming from freer flows in the banking system) is the price to be paid for stronger alignment with the international interest rates, it is perhaps a "transaction" worth considering.

Indian companies operate in a fairly liberal environment for external borrowings. The aggregate cap on external borrowings is high enough and known to be reasonably flexible. At the end of December 2005. ECBs stood at $ 22.4 billion, roughly 19 per cent of total external debt. There are restrictions on the use of these funds and the tenor but this has not been cause for major quibble between Indian industry and the regulators. However, some of the norms for commercial borrowings warrant immediate correction.

First, there is a glaring asymmetry in the way domestic as well as overseas acquisitions are treated under the ECB guidelines. While ECBs are permitted for overseas direct acquisitions or joint ventures, they are not permitted for domestic acquisitions (except for participation in disinvestment). This is an implicit capital control and results in severe financing constraints for domestic acquisitions. This needs to be removed, if indeed the government is interested in fostering a more efficient industrial structure.

The withholding tax regime also works as a selective capital control and skews the incentive structure for borrowing. The average withholding tax on syndicated bank loans works out to 10 per cent, given that most international banks that lend to Indian borrowers are domiciled in countries with which India has tax treaties. However, the withholding tax on debt issues by Indian companies is significantly higher and jacks up the coupon rate. This leads to a bias against bond issuance and a preference for bank loans. The problem with this incentive structure is that most banks are unwilling to lend for more than five years while the funding needs of most Indian companies are typically longer term. The appetite for longer-term debt is really confined to the international debt market. As the infrastructure investments pick up and the appetite for longer-term debt intensifies, the impact of this bias could intensify. It is imperative that the withholding tax rate be reduced and a market for long-dated Indian bonds be allowed to develop globally.

The financial market practitioners argue for using enhanced CAC to foster institutional development in the domestic capital markets. The case of the equity markets is a useful precedent. Few can doubt the fact that with the development of a robust derivatives market, comprehensive dematerialisation of equity holdings, etc, India is on a par with the most developed international markets. One cannot also deny the fact that the presence of FIIs has helped accelerate the pace of market development and structural reform in this market.

Rupee Debt Market

The clear laggard among the domestic capital markets is the rupee debt market, particularly the corporate debt market. The number of actively traded securities in this market is minuscule, volumes are low and institutional improvement virtually absent. One of the notable differences between the equity markets and the local currency debt market is the low ceiling on foreign investment in the latter ($ 2 billion in the government securities market and $1.5 billion in the corporate debt market).

The central bank's discomfort with greater foreign holdings of domestic debt is understandable to a degree. Most crisis-hit economies share a common feature—the presence of large foreign liabilities on their balance sheets. However, given the current level of foreign exchange reserves, the discomfort should have eased a little. In fact, issuing local currency debt has one critical advantage—it does not lead to the dollarisation of liabilities unlike dollar debt contracted through ECBs or NRI dollar deposits.

In short, unlike dollar debt, the currency risk on rupee debt is borne by foreign investors. This itself can work as a safeguard against a sudden flight of capital. In fact, the literature on currency crises shows that it was not just the quantum of foreign holdings of debt that was the culprit—it was the large fraction of "dollarised liabilities" that played an equally critical role. Following this logic, the extreme view would be that foreign currency loans such as ECBs should be discouraged and rupee debt holdings stepped up.

Given this analytical case for taking on more "non-dollarised" foreign liabilities, most financial market practitioners would counsel a very careful, nuanced approach to opening up the corporate debt market. Experience has shown that the existing limits have been used by pure arbitrageurs who have chosen to periodically park their funds at the short end of the yield curve to exploit transitory arbitrage gains. They have not contributed to the development of a more robust trading environment, nor are their investment decisions based on the need to take a larger exposure to India's domestic fundamentals.

A sensible strategy to use FII investments to develop the fixed-income market would increase not only the limit on investments, but also the minimum tenor of bonds that they can invest in. Thus, foreign investors could be excluded from treasury bills and other short-term instruments like commercial paper. If much larger flows are allowed into medium- and long-term bonds, it would help improve the trading environment in the secondary market and also the liquidity in primary issues. This could be the first step towards creating a market in rupee bonds where foreign companies could also list their securities. This ties in with the plan for developing a regional financial hub in India.

Of course, foreign investors would be interested in these products only if they could hedge both currency and interest rate risks. The FIIs are now allowed to hedge their risk to a large extent through currency swaps, options and other derivative instruments. Their alternatives in hedging interest rate risk are considerably more limited and confined to the Overnight Indexed Swaps. Instruments such as interest rate futures will have to be introduced quickly if this market is to develop fast enough.

Finally, the new policy on special economic zones (SEZs) envisages the creation of international financial centres (IFCs) within the SEZs. Banks, through their offshore banking units (OBUs), are expected to play a critical role in developing these centres. These OBUs have been given considerable freedom on the liabilities side of their balance sheet and are free from statutory obligations (cash reserve ratio, statutory liquidity ratio and priority sector obligations). On the asset side, however, they are restricted to being bankers to the production units within the SEZs since 75 per cent of their loans have to go to these units. If the IFCs are to develop as global or regional hubs, the OBUs must be given greater freedom to do business in international markets. It is quite likely that the entities within the SEZs will be some of the key clients of the OBUs but the choice must be left to the banks.

Conclusion

This essay will conclude with the issue of allowing higher outflows of capital under a freer CAC. The focus of CAC until now has really been on increasing flows of capital into the domestic markets (through equity flows, commercial borrowings, etc) and then recently on giving Indian companies greater degrees of freedom for operating in international markets. The policy-makers have perhaps consciously de-emphasised the role of CAC in allowing portfolio diversification of domestic individuals and companies. However, the upswing in economic activity has translated into substantial wealth generation in the domestic economy. In the absence of greater freedom to broaden their asset portfolios, a large fraction of the newly created wealth has been channelled back into local markets, leading to "overheating" and creation of asset bubbles. Thus, even from the perspective of mitigating risk in the domestic economy, more freedom for outflows is desirable.

Some investment channels have, no doubt, been opened up, but have not seen an overwhelming response. For instance, the facility for individuals to hold foreign currency deposits of up to $ 25,000 has hardly been utilised. Individuals have also not come forward in large numbers to invest the $ 25,000 permitted in foreign shares or immovable property. One clear reason is that the mismatch between the needs of the profile of domestic individuals who would potentially invest in this. The central bank should also recognise the fact that it is essentially high net worth individuals who would potentially utilise these channels. Given their income and wealth profiles they are interested in bigger ticket transactions. Thus, if indeed, the objective is to encourage risk diversification, the limit on these outflows should be raised to at least $ 1,00,000.

As far as mutual funds investment in foreign debt is concerned, the 2006-07 budget has announced some critical changes. The most critical change comes in the form of the removal of the apparently innocuous condition of the reciprocal limits of 10 per cent on investments made by the domestic mutual funds in securities abroad. This would enhance the prospect of portfolio diversification considerably. The current limit on investments overseas is $ 2 billion. Some escalation of this limit going forward is desirable.

The majority of practitioners support the measured pace with which the capital account has been opened up in India and would, at best, counsel a moderate acceleration of this pace. However, they would argue for a rationalisation of the existing system of controls to remove the "inefficiencies" within the system. The move to CAC need not be a grand policy gesture—but a steady and focused approach is.

6

Convertibility and Reforms

This article briefly reviews the reforms in the external sector over the last few years, assesses the market response, and examines the possible threats that we need to be conscious of in moving towards fuller convertibility on the capital account (CAC). The first part of the essay deals with reforms so far and their bearing on CAC; the second part analyses the market response and exchange rate movements in the context of CAC. The third and final part uses some of the learning from recent crises—particularly the south-east Asian crisis—to assess where India stands vis-a-vis certain risk factors.

Reforms in the External Sector

The economic reforms, which were initiated in 1991 with the two-step devaluation of the rupee, progressed along two paths. The first path entailed the process of liberalisation—deregulation and phasing out of controls encompassing the entire economy, such as delicensing of industry, eliminating control of capital issues, deregulation of interest rates, relaxing various exchange control measures, etc. The second path was to pursue structural reforms, institutionalising policy changes, refining economic processes, and redefining regulatory and supervisory roles of the government and the central bank. The process of liberalisation enlarged the space for private enterprise, accelerated globalisation of domestic markets and exposed Indian industry to newer threats and opportunities.

The structural reforms, on the other hand, were necessary for an orderly transformation of the economy, and to ensure that the liberalisation process became irreversible (independent of political exigencies) and without destabilising the financial markets. New institutions were created both in public and private sectors, largely on public initiative, which included Securities Exchange Board of India (SEBI), National Stock Exchange (NSE), National Securities Depository (NSDL), Clearing Corporation of India (CCIL), credit rating agencies and primary dealers. Privatisation of public utilities necessitated regulatory authorities for telecom, electricity insurance, etc, with a fair degree of autonomy. Self-regulatory organisations such as Foreign Exchange Dealer's Association of India (FEDAI), Fixed Income Money Market and Derivatives Association of India (FIMMDA) and Association of Mutual Funds in India (AMFI) became increasingly important in financial markets. The new institutions created and supported new processes relating to dematerialisation of securities, electronic trading and real time payment and settlement systems.

Reforms in the external sector were part of the overall economic reforms, which were underpinned by the institutional changes described above. The first reforms were focused en reducing the controls on the rupee's exchange rate. Following the recommendations of the High Level Committee on Balance of Payments, headed by Rangarajan, this phase culminated in August 1994, when the rupee was made fully convertible on the current account under Article VIII of the Articles of Agreement of the IMF.

The next nodal point was the setting up of the first Tarapore committee under the chairmanship of the then deputy governor of the RBI, S.S. Tarapore, which was mandated to create a road map to capital account convertibility. The committee, which submitted its report in

June 1997, recommended a three-year timeframe for complete convertibility, subject to meeting certain preconditions. The preconditions included reduction in the inflation rate to the 3-5 per cent band, reduction in gross non-performing assets (NPAs) of public sector banks to 5 per cent, reduction in the cash reserve ratio to the minimum of 3 per cent, reduction in debt service ratio to 20 per cent, etc. The committee prescribed four indicators to evaluate the adequacy of foreign exchange reserves to safeguard against any contingency and also laid down a phased liberalisation of controls on capital flows.

While the south-east Asian crisis in late 1997 slowed down the reforms, almost all of the benchmarks and preconditions set by Tarapore I have since been met/or exceeded, except for the gross fiscal deficit as a percentage of GDP, which also appears to be very near to the targeted level of 3.5 percent. Since 1997, the structural reforms directly bearing upon CAC fall into three categories: those relating to capital flows, in trade related areas, and reforms leading to market risk management, particularly in the derivative segment.

Investment related reforms: FDI is actually under the purview of government of India and RBI is only the implementing agency. Most sectors of economy have been already opened to foreign investment, with only six prohibited sectors and only a few sectors—e.g., insurance, banking and telecom, which have caps of below 50 per cent.

FIIs are permitted to invest freely in equity markets, subject to sectoral caps. FII investment in the debt market, however, is capped at $ 1.5 billion for corporate bonds and $ 2 billion for government securities. A cap on this segment is felt necessary pending full convertibility, in order to reduce the interest arbitrage between the two currencies.

Indian companies may raise capital globally through very liberal American depository receipts/global depository receipts guidelines and/or up to $ 500 million through the external commercial borrowings (ECBs)/foreign currency convertible bonds window. There are certain restrictions on ECBs, in terms of maturity, end-use and pricing, all of which are not unreasonable (see below) but may be ready for some further liberalisation now. Indian companies may also invest overseas direct investment (ODI) freely (the only exceptions being in the real estate and banking sectors) to the extent of 200 per cent of their net worth. This is perhaps the loudest element of capital flow liberalisation, and the window that is clamouring for more.

Trade related reforms: With the rupee fully convertible on the current account, these reforms pertain mainly to terms of trade—maximum credit for exports is now permitted beyond one year, while for imports credit beyond one year is subject to approval of the RBI. RBI has permitted issue of financial guarantees/letters of comfort by Indian banks to secure trade credit; this and the roll-over of credit on such terms helped many companies to drastically reduce their import costs. Reforms related to risk management: While RBI has been continuously pushing banks to enhance their risk management processes—from detailed ALM guidelines in 1997 to Basel II guidelines (as recently as last month)—their efforts to develop a deep and liquid derivatives market, which is a necessary condition for effective risk management, has not been as successful as it should.

Rupee interest rate swaps were first permitted in 1998, followed by rupee options in 2002. An attempt to launch interest rate futures in 2003 was still-born.

More inexplicably, RBI's restriction on the use of Mumbai interbank forward offer rate (MIFOR), which had evolved as the only tentative term money market benchmark, has dealt a body blow to the evolution of genuine hedging markets. This remains the key lacuna that needs to be addressed in going forward to CAC.

In several cases the reforms have resulted in conditions that met or exceeded the levels suggested by the Tarapore I. For instance, today ODI is permitted up to twice the company's net worth as opposed to Tarapore I's recommendation of $ 50 million in the first phase. As recommended, universal banks have come into existence in place of financial institutions. However, there are still several recommendations (pertaining to overseas investments by individuals and mutual funds, overseas borrowings by Indian banks, flexibility of operations to exporters, etc) that are yet to be implemented.

Of course, 2006 is a world apart from 1997—both from the point of view of global markets and India's new economic confidence and institutionalised strength -and it is appropriate to reassess the benchmarks, which explains why the second committee has been constituted. July 31 -the date that Tarapore II submits its report—will provide a clearer picture of the next steps to capital account convertibility.

Behaviour of the Foreign Exchange Market

It seems clear that the domestic forex market has been evolving ahead of the regulators and appears to provide a leading edge to the move towards capital account convertibility.

The domestic inter-bank forex market has grown dramatically since Tarapore I. In the mid-1990s, daily turnover was in the range of $ 1-2 billion per day, providing a multiplier of around 3 to 4 on underlying trade transactions. Today, daily volumes are around $ 12-13 billion a day, and provide a multiplier of about 17-18 on underlying trade. Global markets trade at 85-90 times the underlying trade, so, while we have moved quite well, it is clear that there is still a long way to go.

The microstructure of the market, too, has changed. While in 1997, the total market volume was about evenly divided between spot and forwards, today, the forward market is about twice the spot market volume. Further, today there is "reasonably good" liquidity in USD/INR options, with market volumes averaging around $ 250 million a day—significantly, though, there are banks reporting that it is sometimes possible to push through $ 100-150 million quite easily on a good day.

However, regulation on the derivatives side—see above—has remained overly heavy-handed, which has limited the growth in derivative volumes, both in options and in interest rate swaps, the market for which is even more stunted. Further, there is a need to consolidate regulation—RBI regulates the over-the-counter (OTC) market, in which banks trade spot and forward foreign exchange, options and interest rate swaps; on the other hand, interest rate futures, which admittedly have not yet got off the ground, but in which banks would be significant players, were intended to be regulated by SEBI.

Again, on the structural side, in the early to mid-1990s, voice brokers were the main intermediaries in the inter-bank market; however, with Reuters' dealing and other electronic brokers coming into the market in a big way, the bulk of transactions are now conducted electronically with voice brokers capturing perhaps 15 per cent of the volumes. It is significant, however, that voice brokers are most active when market volatility spikes, since "market intelligence" comes at a premium at that time. Obviously, brokers are more active in the less liquid segments, like forwards and, more recently, options. RBI needs to empower brokers to a greater extent to drive volumes in the derivative segment, particularly as there remains a huge diversity of knowledge levels between different market players.

In fact, as in the case of regulation of banking activity, there is considerable confusion on the regulation of brokers. Forex and forex derivatives brokers report in to FEDAI, whereas money market and gilts brokers report in to FIMMDA. There is no clarity on brokerage in interest rate swaps, which often straddle both markets, and currency derivatives, which would provide an excellent half-way house to capital account convertibility. This would also fall between the two pillars of regulation.

Despite all this confusion, the spot USD/ INR market, as mentioned earlier, has been making steady strides towards freedom. Not only have daily volumes risen to "respectable" levels, market volatility, particularly over the past year, has risen as well, to an average of around 6 per cent, from average levels of around 2 per cent in previous years.

More importantly, the volatility has become more stable in the past year, with RBI less frantic to control intra- or inter-day movements. In times past, RBI would step in to discipline the market if the rupee moved by even a few paise in a day. Today, however, we find 10 to 20 paise (0.2 to 0.5 per cent) intra-day movements quite commonplace. As a result, the difference (in percentage terms) between the peak and average volatility of the rupee has become much more stable. The chart shows how this parameter has moved since June 2002 for the rupee, the Thai baht, the Singapore dollar and the euro. Using this as a measure of market development, the Indian forex market is far more developed than the Thai market and even comes in a bit better than the Singapore dollar. It has a long way to go to get to the fully liquid conditions that obtain for the euro, but clearly, the Indian forex market is on its way.

Challenges

There are, of course, concerns that moving to full convertibility of currency could lead to problems in the financial markets. These concerns are based on the experiences of various debt and payment crises faced by emerging market countries in the post-Bretton Woods era. The widespread Latin-American and Nigerian default in the 1980s, the Argentinian crisis of early 1990s (which had a dramatic revival that was reversed by a repeat crisis in early 21st century), the Mexican crisis of mid-1990s, south-east Asian crisis of 1997, closely followed by collapse of Russian markets point out the vulnerability of emerging markets, often in the wake of financial deregulation and liberalisation of exchange controls.

Various studies have shown that poor financial infrastructure (which resulted in both high-risk lending and over borrowing), low returns on investment, implicit guarantees by the state, speculative boom in equity and real estate markets and inadequacies in macroeconomic policy constitute the recurring theme throughout the financial crises over the last two decades. Interestingly, imbalances in government finances, though an obvious suspect, are not seen as a major driver of crises, unless, of course, the imbalances are huge and growing—a situation that does not describe India today. In fact, in most of these areas. India is reasonably well placed. Financial infrastructure: As described earlier, Indian institutional restructuring has been comprehensive. SEBI and stock exchanges have been developing sound risk management practices. Banking supervision has been strengthened with a focus on market risk management. Provisioning norms, capital adequacy and accounting practices conform to global standards. The entry of foreign banks and investment institutions have strengthened competition in the market. The only area where we need to further evolve is with regard to derivative products. Overborrowing: Though there has been a spurt in ECBs recently, foreign debt is less than our forex reserves, and external debt in proportion to GDP at below 25 per cent is quite comfortable, as compared to, say, 45-60 per cent in the case of Malaysia, Indonesia and Thailand (MIT) just before the crisis. This suggests that we need to be cautious about removing the overall ceiling on ECB. Short-term debt as at end-December 2005 was less than 7 per cent of foreign reserves—again, this compares well with Thailand's 122 per cent and Indonesia's near-300 per cent right before the crisis. Clearly, we have very little to be concerned about in this regard.

Returns on investment: Corporate India is going through a boom cycle and earnings are at historic highs. The return on capital employed for the top 500 companies as at end-December 2006 amounted to 25 per cent. Return on equity of companies with FDI for the year 2003-04 was 18.4 per cent as compared to 17.2 per cent in the previous year (RBI survey). Clearly, the economy is strong and, as such, would be a good time to take aggressive steps.

The government of India no longer guarantees commercial borrowings by public sector under takings or banks. While there is implicit support from the government, it is believed that PSUs have been able to borrow on their own strength. The government, however, may not allow any major bank to fail, whether in the public or private sector. There is some more work to be done in this area, but we believe, given the current strength of the economy, this is a moot point at the moment. Speculative boom: The Sensex as at end March

2006 has grown by 72 per cent over January 2005 level and it is not clear how long the levels will be sustained. However, the growth is apparently supported by higher corporate earnings and the ascendancy was fairly well sustained over last few months. Current P/E is around 20, but the market had earlier seen levels above 24. Real estate on the other hand paints a more worrisome picture. Real estate prices have shown an increase of 60 per cent to 100 per cent in the metros and some of the high end investment could be speculative.

However, the speculative boom either in stock markets or in real estate is unlikely to affect the stability of financial markets as the exposure of banks to both the sectors is strictly controlled by RBI—note, in particular, RBI's increase in risk provisioning norms in the last monetary policy.

Macroeconomic policy: Macroeconomic policies have long ceased to be protective, with opening of economy and adherence to WTO agreements. Fiscal policies are clearly aiming at reducing the deficit to below 3 per cent of GDP. The central bank has operational autonomy and monetary policies are largely devoid of political influence.

In sum, we would say that the Indian economy seems very comfortably placed with respect to these risk factors.

There are, of course, some concerns with respect to global and domestic imbalances. Global imbalances are today largely about high and volatile oil prices and the possibility of a sharp rise in US interest rates to support the dollar in the event of a collapse (which could trigger significant outflows from emerging markets including India). In our view, the underlying Strength of the Indian economy is more than sufficient to sustain any shocks here. Of course, if global growth drops sharply, we will be affected, but not any more so is as a result of having a substantially more open capital account. In fact, in the event that the resolution of global imbalances (if and when it happens) results in a collapse of the dollar, India could actually benefit from increased capital flows.

Domestic imbalances, however, are another issue, and mainly relate to sectoral growth differences and social inequities. While these may not have a direct bearing on CAC, their political impact can create greater volatility in a more open financial environment. Of course, this is not to suggest that these concerns should slow down the move towards capital account convertibility, the bottom line of which is a substantial increase in the efficiency of the Indian economy. It is rather to point out that Tarapore II should—and, considering its composition, likely will—focus as much on the real economy as on financial markets in laying down an express road map.

Conclusion

There is little doubt that moving towards a more open capital account would benefit the country enormously; amongst others, here are some of the key issues we feel Tarapore II should address,

(i) *Residual controls on FDI/ECB need to be removed:* In particular, global issuers and investors should have free access to the rupee debt market, so as to make rupee debt paper globally tradable even before fuller CAC is achieved (as in the case of ADR/GDR issues). This is perhaps the right time to take the step, as ADB is proposing to issue rupee debt of 1,320 crore. Banks and non-bank infrastructure finance companies may be provided free access to ECB/global debt issues, within the overall ceiling of ECB; RBI may prescribe eligibility norms in terms of financial strength of the Indian issuers, in order to avoid credit default.

(ii) *Taxation:* Tax laws and stamp duty must be simplified without scope for ambiguity. Removal of withholding tax on long-term investments (FDI) and borrowings (ECB) would incidentally help create a global finance centre in India. All fiscal issues relating to debt market should be held exclusively in the central list.

(iii) *Social Equity:* Sectoral imbalances in the economy need to be addressed seriously. Corporate finance to agriculture needs to be encouraged: credit insurance to agriculture and SMEs would also provide them easier access to institutional credit. Credit derivatives will become imperative for hedging corporate as well as non-corporate credit risks. Some affirmative action by the government may become necessary in the initial stages.

7

Indian Story of Convertibility

Capital account convertibility (CAC) occupied centre stage for about six years after India announced in 1994 her readiness to accept the obligations that entail external current account convertibility. For some curious reason, the issue almost disappeared from the reforms radar till late March 2005 when prime minister Manmohan Singh asked the ministry of finance and the Reserve Bank of India (RBI) to revisit the theme of CAC. The RBI has since constituted a committee to set out a road map to fuller CAC. The composition of the committee, however, is in line with the RBI's penchant to appoint more or less the same persons in most of the committees.1

The terms of reference of the committee are: (i) to review the experience of various measures of capital account liberalisation in India; (ii) to examine implications of fuller CAC on monetary and exchange rate management, financial markets and the financial system; (iii) to study the implications of dollarisation in India of domestic assets and liabilities and Intel-nationalisation of the Indian rupee; (iv) to provide a comprehensive medium term operational framework, with sequencing and timing, for fuller CAC taking into account the above implications and progress in revenue and fiscal deficits of both the centre and states; (v) to survey regulatory framework in countries which have advanced towards fuller CAC; (vi) to suggest appropriate policy measures and prudential safeguards to ensure monetary and financial stability; and (vii) to make such other recommendations as the committee may deem relevant to the subject. The committee is to commence its work from May 1, 2006 and is expected to submit its report by July 31, 2006.

In this article, we shall first provide a snapshot picture of the various measures undertaken in the area of exchange management and exchange control since the publication of report of the Committee on Capital Account Convertibility in 1997 (to be henceforth referred to Tarapore I). This we believe is necessary if one were to make a determination as to whether there should be fuller capital account convertibility. We shall set out to undertake this task and then discuss the policy choices available at the present time.

Background

It would be legitimate to expect that in the Tarapore II report, there will be discussion on the actions that have so far been taken on the recommendations of Tarapore I, but that may not by itself be interesting for two reasons. First, it is necessary to ask some searching questions as to whether the Tarapore I recommendations were in fact based on a good data base, sound empirical methodology and testing, besides analytics. Next, the economic circumstances in which the Indian economy is presently placed and the international perceptions about the need for a full CAC are very different from those in the mid-1990s. It must be noted that Tarapore I was submitted at the end of May 1997, before the onset of the east Asian currency and banking crises. The east Asian crises and subsequent crises in Latin America have shown that fuller C AC is neither necessary nor sufficient for achieving higher growth and economic stability.

The terms of reference now given would require Tarapore II to collect information about relevant international experiences as well as conduct a number of econometric tests—such as sensitivity and stress tests—besides the probability of occurrence of the expected outcomes of the measures that are theoretically recommended for implementation as part of fuller CAC and to empirically establish the realism behind the road map it is expected to recommend.

Structural reforms formed the central component of the new policy regime established in India from 1991 onwards. They focused on progressive liberalisation of the trade and payments regime particularly after the introduction of a unified exchange rate system in March 1993. Initially (i.e., till early 1997), the capital account liberalisation (CAL) process began with relaxation of rules relating to foreign direct investment, portfolio investment by foreign institutional investors, access for the Indian corporate entities to overseas financial markets in the form of global depository receipts (GDRs) and foreign currency convertible bonds (FCCBs), deposits for non-resident Indians (NRIs), and access to external commercial borrowings (ECBs). In August 1994, the country accepted the obligations under Article VIII of the Articles of Agreement of the International Monetary Fund (IMF) and thus ensured that current account convertibility for both inflows and outflows was secured.

It is important to note that once a member accepts the obligations under Article VIII, it cannot reverse its action. But India's entry into the list of countries under Article VIII was characterised by a few unresolved issues. One of the unresolved issues related to the transfer of amortisation payments on loans by non-resident relatives. Yet another one related to the repatriation of property income of NRIs and deposits with Indian companies of NRIs and overseas corporate bodies (OCBs) that were on a non-repatriation basis. The understanding in August 1994 was that repatriation on this account would be permitted in a phased manner over a three-year period. Current payments on advertisements in foreign television media were not permitted, a restriction that was removed only in February 2004. Again, foreign investors could repatriate dividends net of taxes on the condition that over a five-year period, an amount equivalent to the repatriated dividends is made good through export earnings, a restriction that had come to be known as "dividend balancing" and that was dispensed with after considerable pressure from foreign investors with effect from November 5, 1999.

Current account convertibility together with other reforms gave much confidence to foreign investors about the prospects of the Indian economy. Total foreign investments which were about $ 559 million in 1992-93 went up to $ 6,133 million by the close of 1996-97—the year that was the base for the recommendations of Tarapore I. Current account deficit as proportion of India's GDP which was 1.7 per cent in 1992-93 was 1.2 per cent by 1996-97. Foreign exchange reserves that stood at $9,832 million at the end of 1992-93 moved up to $ 26,423 million.

The CAL measures taken since the submission of Tarapore I report have been substantial as could be seen from their listing in the annexure of the annual reports of the Reserve Bank of India. They are characterised by gradualism in that the quantitative ceilings in respect of certain items (say in respect of foreign direct investment as per cent of paid up capital of Indian corporate entities) have been increased. Gradualism could be also seen in a number of other measures where quantitative ceilings cannot be applied (as for example in regard to investments by Indian corporate bodies and resident individuals). The measures cover a wide range.

Listing out the measures in a chronological order is not attempted in this paper. Such an approach would be required if one were to know as to: (i) how the process of gradualism took place and (ii) what has prompted the authorities to introduce liberalisation measures in modest doses at different points in time. Our purpose here is to have an idea of CAL that has already taken place and the main considerations that underlie them. We shall accordingly provide only a few measures for illustrative purposes.

Liberalisation of Exchange Control

The main areas of focus of CAL are: (a) external commercial borrowings (ECBs); (b) foreign investment; (c) non-resident deposits; (d) Indian corporate investments abroad; (e) relaxations given to authorised dealers and banks in India; (f) transactions relating to resident Indians; and (g) others. ECBs in the Indian context should be understood to refer to loans taken from foreign markets/entities abroad, FCCBs. leasing, floating rate notes (FRNs), trader credits and self-liquidating loans. Foreign investments cover both foreign direct investment and portfolio investments made by foreign institutional investors (FIIs). NRIs and OCBs could also take part in foreign investment besides foreign investors and firms abroad. NRIs at times get clubbed together with persons of Indian origin (PIO). Investments by Indian corporate entities would include manufacturing entities, service providers, banks and other financial institutions. Resident Indians are Indian nationals residing in India for at least six months at a stretch in a year. The residual category, namely, others include transactions relating to gold, financial markets and mutual funds.

The gradual approach implies steady increases in the ceilings or caps on the amounts that can be borrowed or repatriated. This is guided by the consideration that external debt should be within sustainable limits. The gradual approach also implies that countries would place restrictions on the terms and conditions of capital transactions. Ever since the east Asian crisis in 1997, countries have been cautious in incurring short-term external liabilities for the fear that increase in such liabilities would send signals to foreign investors of stress and in some cases of vulnerability to speculative attacks. Thus, for example, the ceiling for ECB in India is at present placed at $ 500 million or equivalent with a minimum average maturity of five years under the automatic route. If the average maturity is lower, say three to five years, the ceiling placed is mere $ 20 million. In respect of trade, credits, the maturity period is one year, and the amounts under this category can only be up to $ 20 million.

Keeping in view the need to reduce external debt liabilities, Indian companies have been allowed to convert ECBs into equity subject to certain conditions. Moreover, Indian companies can prepay the ECBs under the automatic route and the existing FCCBs.

In the case of FDI, the gradual approach in India implies not only sectoral limits but also gradual extension of items/areas where FDI is permitted. For instance, under the RBI automatic route, FDI is allowed in all activities excepting in a few items. This is the case also in respect of NRI/OCB investments. In respect of FIIs, the limits are on their aggregate investments as well as on an individual FII investment in a company. For instance, the aggregate holding of all FIIs/sub-accounts of FIIs should not exceed 24 per cent of the paid up capital of a company, but this limit could be increased up to 49 per cent by the Indian company if the general body passes a resolution to that effect. The ceiling for investment by a single FII in a company is 10 per cent of the total paid up capital. FIIs have been given some flexibility as well as prudential support in that their total investment has been placed in terms of two components—equity and debt instruments—in the ratio of 70:30. NRI deposits have all been now rendered repatriable. Non-resident ordinary accounts. however, can be held by NRIs with residents.

The CAL in India is also characterised by measures that broaden and strength linkages with the international markets through permissions granted to Indian companies and authorised dealers (ADs) and banks to invest abroad. In the case of ADs and banks, CAL measures have also been informed of prudential considerations as well as liquidity positions. Thus for example, Indian companies can invest in rated bonds/fixed income securities up to certain limits. They can also invest in the overseas financial sector. They can invest up to 100 per cent of their net worth by way of market purchase for investment in a foreign entity without any limit to the amount of such investment. Indian companies with overseas offices can also acquire immovable properties abroad for their business or for staff residential purposes. ADs can borrow foreign currencies from their head offices or branches or co-respondents outside India up to 25 per cent of their unimpaired tier I capital or $ 10 million, whichever is higher. ADs can invest in overseas money market/debt instruments provided they are of sovereign issue with high rating and with residual maturity of less than one year. Indian banks can invest undeployed FCNR (B) funds in overseas markets in long-term fixed income securities with high ratings. The CAL measures also provided for hedging against currency risks and price risks.

The general perception in India is that CAL measures have not taken into account the foreign exchange needs of resident Indians. This perception has arisen partly because resident Indians have been given the lowest priority in the sequencing of CAL. At present, resident Indians are given permission to remit foreign exchange for employment abroad, emigration, maintenance of close relatives abroad, education, and medical treatment. The limit in this regard is placed uniformly at $ 1,00,000 based on simple self-declaration. Resident employees of software companies can purchase foreign securities under the ADR/GDR linked stock option scheme up to $ 50,000 in a block of five calendar years. Residents can open, hold and maintain current accounts in foreign currency in India out of the foreign exchange acquired by them. They can also retain foreign exchange in cash or travellers cheques up to $ 2,000. They can also invest in rated bonds/fixed income securities abroad up to certain limits and under certain conditions. They can borrow interest free loans up to $ 2,50,000 from their close relatives resident outside India on repatriation basis with a maturity of over one year. Residents can hold international credit cards for use in India or abroad subject to certain regulations.

The Future Policy Choices

The CAL measures undertaken so far have taken care of almost all the exchange requirements of foreign investors and NRIs. One has not come across any serious complaints from foreign investors or NRIs about exchange restrictions relevant for them. The foreign exchange requirements of ADs and commercial banks and resident Indians too have been served well by the CAL measures as seen from the above listing. In general, the space between the actual amount of CAL and fuller CAC is small. India, one could argue, has almost arrived at the doorsteps of full CAC.

This does not mean that all the areas for CAL have been exhausted. For example, one can examine the possibility of having foreign currency bonds issued by corporate entities to resident Indians—an area that has not been so far opened. Again, one can explore as to whether non-residents can participate directly in the public sector's divestment process without any limit. Moreover, the definition of ADs itself could be widened to accommodate all India financial institutions and other financial institutions that are being closely monitored by regulators from the point of view of prudential compliance.

One would be tempted to know as to whether this is the opportune time to declare fuller CAC. For the policy authorities, this is only one dimension of the policy-making process even though there is a general market perception that given the buoyancy of stock markets, the large foreign exchange assets, and the generally good economic prospects, full-scale CAC should be undertaken. It is, however, possible that policy authorities would deliberately choose to maintain the status quo. That is, the current gradualist approach on CAC would be continued. This policy choice could be treated as an independently determined one. Or, it could be in association with the stipulation about meeting some predetermined preconditions for implementing fuller CAC. This would imply that one could, as a matter of policy, consider having fuller CAC once the preconditions are met. Yet another policy option would be to bid goodbye to gradualism and quickly move to fuller CAC say within a few months. Finally, policy authorities could consider having a definitive road map to fuller CAC, the option that would be the subject of inquiry by Tarapore II. Laying down a road map would not, however, preclude a gradualist approach or setting up preconditions. The preconditions could be in the nature of reiteration of what had been spelt out in Tarapore I report or in the nature of additions or variations of the preconditions that were enumerated in Tarapore I report.

None of the policy alternatives question the desirability of fuller CAC or in the least a well-stacked CAL. The theoretical stand is essentially in favour of capital account convertibility for augmenting efficiency and growth.4 Informational problems could however come in the way of efficiency but transparency practices, knowledge revolution and market regulations including risk management strategies could restrict adverse selection, moral hazard and disorderly volatility and help attain the second best.

The empirical evidence on fuller CAC is not decisive. Countries that have liberalised capital movements along with implementation of prudential policies and sound institutional framework have posted better economic outcomes than those that did not provide supplemental policy and institutional support to capital A Short Guide to Policy Determination

The desirability of having fuller CAC should be viewed not merely from the point of view of the current or even estimated inflation rates, foreign exchange reserves, current account and fiscal deficits, and non-performing assets of the banking system as the preconditions approach envisages, but also from the viewpoint of the institutional framework that is being continuously improved and the potential growth of the economy based on the productivity gains arising out of adoption of new technologies. Presently, the inflation rates as reflected in the movements of the wholesale price index for all commodities are placed at around 4 per cent per annum. Foreign exchange reserves have gone beyond $150 billion, more than six months of average imports. The current account deficit is presently estimated to be less than 2 per cent of GDP and is consistent with the sustained growth of net capital receipts.5 Fiscal deficit of the centre is in the ball park of 4 per cent of GDP, while non-performing assets of the banking sector are steadily on the decline.

One could argue that the outcomes on preconditions are not exactly in line with what has been recommended by Tarapore I.6 But recommendations about safe or desirable end-period statistics of variables considered to be critical for adoption of CAC should not be considered sacrosanct. In any case, the set of preconditions and the suggested end-period statistics for the pre-conditions are not a part of any internally consistent model in Tarapore I, a point that needs to be kept in view. Now that (a) the actual outcomes are close to the statistical magnitudes given in Tarapore I report, (b) the risk management strategies exist, and (c) the general economic situation is considered good, the determination of the timing of fuller CAC is essentially a matter of policy-makers' judgment.

There has been considerable discussion of India's high potential growth with almost all the estimates of growth ranging from 8 per cent to 10 per cent a year. The projections are based partly on the expected application of new technologies and on the favourable demographic dividend. Insofar as the institutional framework is concerned, one needs to view it in two parts. The first is in terms of the implementation of a number of international standards and codes in the areas of accounting, auditing, transparency practices in fiscal and monetary policies, securities regulation, insurance regulation, banking supervision and regulation, anti-money laundering, payments system and corporate governance. Transmission of assessments of compliance with the standards to the public at large would provide enormous comfort for policy-makers, and keen observers of the Indian economic scene while deciding on fuller CAC. The second part would have to do with the legal support to the institutional and policy framework and processes. There has been strengthening of the institutional framework in India in recent years, with discussions being focused on not only passing of new or amended laws but also on economic governance of all the segments of the financial sector.

Like the national authorities, the international financial community is concerned about crisis prevention in all emerging market economies so that financial stability is secured globally. Both national and international financial communities recognise that financial stability is not guaranteed by either CAC or by capital controls.

Does it mean that a good degree of capital mobility can coexist with exchange rate stability through intervention even when the exchange rate regime is considered flexible? The short answer is yes. Central banks may also have to satisfy themselves with some self-imposed discipline on their autonomy and independence in the conduct of monetary policy. In any case, most emerging market economies manage exchange rates. They also do not have unfettered freedom in the conduct of monetary policy. Under such an environment, establishment of fuller CAC is possible. Determination of fuller CAC in the ultimate analysis is not based on the contemporary thinking of economists: it is essentially led by policy-makers' preferences and judgments.

When did the 'HINDU' Rate of Growth End?

It has been abundantly clear for some time that the institution of economic reforms through a paradigm shift in economic policy in 1991 was followed by an acceleration of the growth rate (Table 1). Such acceleration thus marked an impressive break with the so-called "Hindu" rate of growth of 3.5 per cent and vindicated in the process the faith of the reformers in the efficacy of reforms. However, a new orthodoxy—following the works of Rodrik and Subramanian (2004), Virmani (2004) and Panagariya (2004)—has, meanwhile, emerged that holds that there is nothing unusual about economic growth after 1991-92 since comparable growth rates were witnessed during the 1980s, prior to the 1991 reforms.

New Orthodoxy

Rodrik and Subramanian (2004) question the attribution of India's higher growth rates in the 1990s to economic liberalisation, since similar rates were characteristic of the 1980s, when, in their view, there had been little or no liberalisation. Averring that the transition to higher growth started around 1980, long before the initiation of liberalisation, they hold strongly to. the view that it was generated by attitudinal change—not policy change—on the part of the state to a pro-business (in contrast to a pro-liberalisation or pro-market) approach. Consequently, the change "left little paper trail in actual policies but had an important impact on investors' psychology". For them, "this change was inaugurated with the return of a much-chastened Indira Gandhi to political power in the 1980s" and served as "the essential trigger" for the 1980s economic boom [Rodrik and Subramanian 2004: 3-5, 28].

Virmani's (2004) position is somewhat similar, forcefully maintaining that the structural break to a higher growth rate occurred precisely in 1980. Interestingly, he, too, resolves the paradox of "dramatic changes in the growth rate" amidst little or modest reform by resort to social psychology: "The same leader [Indira Gandhi], who had instituted the earlier control policies that slowed the economy, was changing the direction of economic policy. As she was perceived to have learnt from her own experience, the changes were more credible to both potential beneficiaries and losers" [Virmani 2004: 33-41].

Representing a different position, Panagariya (2004) focuses largely on the period after Rajiv Gandhi's accession to power in 1984 and argues that it was reform activism, indeed, that "played a significant role" in the impressive growth performance during several years prior to the 1991 reforms. Importantly, he holds that the 1980s reforms, because of their demonstrated success, played a foundational role in enacting the 1991 reforms and thus were a "precursor" to the latter. At the same time, in a sweeping assessment that lumps together a vast period but with little systematic specification, Panagariya (2004) differentiates both the 1980s and 1990s reforms from "the isolated and sporadic liberalising actions during 1960s and 1970s, which were often reversed within a short period".

Two propositions clearly stand out in the three studies discussed above. One, that the year 1980 marks a structural break in India's economic growth, with the Hindu rate of growth prevailing before it and the more robust growth coming after it. Even Panagariya—who has methodological reservations about specify ing precisely any particular year as the starting point for growth acceleration during the 1980s -agrees nonetheless that "growth rates between the 1980s and 1990s are comparable". Regardless, the year 1980 seems to have gained considerable acceptance as marking the real initiation of improved growth performance. Two, there is the additional belief that the growth acceleration starting in 1980 is related to the return of Indira Gandhi to power in that year with a suddenly changed ideological position, aiming to move away from her earlier socialist rhetoric or policies. This article takes serious issue with both propositions.

A Revisionist Perspective

It seems that the presumed shift in Indira Gandhi's ideological or policy orientation—invoked by Rodrik and Subramanian (2004) and Virmani (2004) as an explanation for growth acceleration in 1980—appears as a 'deus ex machina' in their studies. They offer no evidence as to when and, more importantly, why the shift in Indira Gandhi's ideological orientation took place. That shift remains essentially un discussed and unexplained. Besides, can these studies be taken as definitive on the point that economic reforms in India did not begin until the 1980s? A little recourse to history -which often has little attraction for most economists—is essential in order to shed light on the question.

Lurch to the Left

With the twin aims of building socialism and economic independence, India launched in 1956, under the aegis of the Second Five-Year Plan (1956-57/1960-61). a gigantic and ambitious import substitution strategy focused on heavy industry, intended to be established basically in the public sector. The Second Plan, however, ran into trouble right from the start because of the twin capital and foreign exchange constraints, and was rescued only through special resource mobilisation by foreign donors. Subsequently, the Third Plan (1961-62/1965-66), which persisted with the heavy industry strategy, was also headed for trouble, fundamentally because of the resource constraint and the imbalanced nature of the economic strategy with its relative neglect of agriculture and consumer goods.

Soon tiring of providing vast amounts of aid with no end in sight, the US successfully pressured India into devaluation in 1966 as part of a liberalisation package. That was in one sense the beginning of economic liberalisation in India, but the effort was soon aborted, because its centre piece, the rupee devaluation, proved to be a veritable disaster.

At that moment, Indian politics took a decisively radical turn to the left led by Indira Gandhi, who split the Congress Party in 1969, but remained at the head of the government with the support of the Communist Party of India (CPI) and some regional parties.

Regardless of what precisely her own ideological views were, Indira Gandhi presided in the next several years over what Nayar has called "the reign of ideology". The trigger in the party split had been her decision to nationalise all the major banks, bringing under public ownership commercial banking covering over 85 per cent of the country's deposits. After the split, the government tightened the screws on the private sector, especially big business, through new and stricter constraints. The Monopolies and Restrictive Trade Practices Act, 1969, barred all business houses with assets of more than Rs200 million from expansion or diversification. The Industrial Licensing Policy was also modified in 1970 to restrict 20 large industrial houses and their individual firms to only "core" industries (new projects worth over Rs50 million). Thus, those in society who had the most capacity to produce and invest were placed in a straitjacket.

Even after Indira Gandhi won the 1971 elections and the government was no longer beholden to the CPI for parliamentary support, as it had been between 1969 and" 1971, socialism remained ascendant. The government continued on the radical path, nationalising the coal industry, general insurance, the copper industry, a significant segment of the steel industry, and a substantial part of the textile industry. Finally, as if in an ideological delirium, the government nationalised the wholesale wheat trade in 1973, aiming eventually to nationalise the entire wholesale food grains trade. In addition, through the Foreign Exchange Regulation Act, 1973, it envisaged coercing fôreign firms in India to reduce their equity to 40 per cent or withdraw from India altogether.

Table 1: GDP Growth Rates 1951-52 To 2004-05

(In per cent)

Year	*GDP*	*Year*	*GDP*	*Year*	*GDP*
1951-52	2.3	1975-76	9.0	1990-91	5.6
1952-53	2.8	1976-77	1.2	1991-92	1.3
1953-54	6.1	1977-78	7.5	1992-93	5.1
1954-55	4.2	1978-79	5.5	1993-94	5.9
1955-56	2.6	1979-80	-5.2	1994-95	7.3
Average	3.6	Average	3.6	Average	5.0
1956-57	5.7	1980-81	7.2	1995-96	7.3
1957-58	-1.2	1981-82	6.0	1996-97	7.8
1958-59	7.6	1982-83	3.1	1997-98	4.8
1959-60	2.2	1983-84	7.7	1998-99	6.5
4-Year	3.6	1984-85	4.3	1999-00	6.1
Average*		Average	5.7	Average	6.5
1960-61	7.1	1985-86	4.5	2000-01	4.4
1961-62	3.1	1986-87	4.3	2001-02	5.8
1962-63	2.1	1987-88	3.8	2002-03	3.8
1963-64	5.1	1988-89	10.5	2003-04	8.5
1964-65	7.6	1989-90	6.7	2004-05	7.5
Average	5.0	Average	6.0	Average	6.0
1965-66	-3.7	2005-06	8.1		
1966-67	1.0				
1967-68	8.0				
1968-69	2.6				
1969-70	6.5				
Average*	2.9				
1970-71	5.0				
1971-72	1.0				
1972-73	-0.3				

1973-74	4.6				
1974-75	1.2				
Average	2.3				
Other averages for select periods					
(a) 1956-57		(d) 1975-76		(h) 1991-92	
to 1974-75	3.4	to 1978-79	5.8	to 2005-06	6.0
(b) 1956-57		(e) 1975-76		(i) 1992-93	
to 1979-80	3.5	to 2005-06	5.6	to 2005-06	6.4
(c) 1965-66		(f) 1980-81		(j) 1992-93	
to 1974-75	2.6	to 1990-91	5.8	to 1996-97	6.7
		(g) 1980-81			
		to 1991-92	5.4		

Note: * The given four-year period starts with 1956-57 when the second five-year plan, focused on heavy industry and the public sector, was launched.

Source: Central Statistical Organisation, National Accounts Statistics 2005, GoI, New Delhi, 2005, Statement S-1.2. For 2000-01 and after, Press Information Bureau, GoI, Press Note, January 31 and February 7, 2006.

Change of Economic Course

What finally brought an end to the nationalisation spree and "the reign of ideology" was a gathering economic crisis in the early 1970s, throwing up challenges to the government on two fronts: soaring inflation amidst widespread scarcities and a sudden and severe deterioration in the balance of payments position. Behind the developing crisis lay multiple causes. Whether or not resulting from the government's hostility toward and restrictions on big business, manufacturing grew at the rate of less than 4 per cent during the first half of the 1970s, which performance was lower than the already depressed rates of the last half of the 1960s. Meanwhile, droughts in 1972 and 1974 ravaged agricultural production, with the average growth rate for the first-half of the 1970s averaging only 1.5 per cent, which was much lower than the population growth rate. The consequence was immense food shortages and a rise in prices. The final coup de grace was delivered by the quadrupling of oil prices by OPEC in 1973. As a result, the dominant characteristic of-the first-half of the 1970s—as earlier in the second-half of the 1960s—was economic stagnation and turmoil. The average GDP growth rate for the former period was an abysmal 2.3 per cent, even lower than the already poor record of 2.9 per cent of the latter period (Table 1). The Hindu growth rate would have, indeed, shone in comparison with such dismal performance. Besides, inflation, which was only 5.6 per cent in 1971-72, rose to 10 per cent the next year, and then soared to 20.2 per cent and 25.2 per cent in the subsequent two years [Joshi and Little 1994:105]. The rising inflation and widespread shortages of essential goods (including food) ravaged the poor, the workers and the middle classes. The massive social discontent resulting from this economic wreckage burst forth into street demonstrations, riots and violence; industrial unrest became widespread. The escalating industrial unrest culminated in an "unprecedented" threat by the two million employees of the government-owned railways to go on strike in May 1974, an action that "promised to destabilise the country" by shutting down the economy altogether [Joshi and Little 1994:54-55]. Meanwhile, seeking to exploit the social discontent, opposition parties mounted a major offensive against the government and transformed the situation into a political crisis. Economic destabilisation threatened to escalate into political destabilisation.

Late 1973 marked a turning point. The government decided to jettison its earlier radical and populist thrust of imposing restrictions on the private sector and of relentlessly expanding the public sector. It now opted for a growth-oriented approach. Critical to the government's change of course was its revised assessment about the results of the series of radical policies that it had pursued over the preceding half decade. Indira Gandhi had apparently become disillusioned about the radical course, especially after the fiasco that had followed on the food front in the wake of the government's takeover of the wholesale wheat trade. Jha (1980:171) refers to "the suspicion that grew in Mrs Gandhi that she had been made use of by the communists and their fellow travellers in the Congress to pass legislation whose effect was to disrupt production, without making society significantly more egalitarian". The oil price shocks highlighted for Indira Gandhi and her government the fact that the thrust on insulation from the world economy had not only been futile but also injurious.

In January 1974, the government rescinded its takeover of the wholesale wheat trade, marking the first reversal in the relentless expansion of control by the state over the market. Then it signalled its new economic course by savage action on the labour front in the belief that inflation had already reached intolerable levels and wage concessions were therefore no longer politically acceptable. In May, it ruthlessly crushed the threatened railway strike by large-scale arrests of trade union leaders and workers. Any pretensions to socialism were thus really buried in these quite brutal actions against labour, even if the rhetoric about socialism lingered on. Finally, the government adopted a deflationary policy package in July 1974, which shifted the focus of economic policy from the pursuit of social justice and socialism to economic orthodoxy. There can be no doubt that it was the severe economic crisis of the early 1970s that induced the government to take recourse to economic orthodoxy and to resort to the liberalisation cure, howsoever mild in form. It changed economic course by resorting to a set of more orthodox measures, which constituted a radical departure from the path that it had pursued in recent years. If policy reversal has the potential for enhancing credibility about reform, as Virmani maintains, then it actually took place in 1974. At the heart of the policy shift was the abysmal growth performance over the previous decade and its social and political consequences.

Incipient Liberalisation

What the government essentially did in the face of the enormous economic crisis was to turn to economic reform, including adopting an economic stabilisation package. The crushing of the railway strike in June 1974 was the opening move in the attack on inflation, in that it prevented demand from escalating further and preempted wage demands from labour in other areas of the economy. The government followed up this tough action with equally stern measures in the areas of taxes, wages and prices. In combination with changes in fiscal and monetary policy, these drastic measures proved extremely efficacious. With prices beginning to fall by October, the cycle of inflation had been broken. The trend continued into the next fiscal year, so that the wholesale price index for 1975-76 was 1 per cent below that for 1974-75.

On the external front, the government obtained no-conditionality or low-conditionality loans from the IMF, with the largest amount coming from the new oil facility. Explicit devaluation was politically unacceptable. But the government really needed no action on thi s front except to quietly continue with the creeping devaluation that resulted from linking the rupee in late 1971 to a weak sterling, and the value of the rupee fell by 20 per cent between 1971 and 1975. While overt devaluation was avoided, covert devaluation was sustained, with the result that exports (including manufactures) got a boost despite the economic stagnation, industrial slowdown and the gathering economic crisis.

Through the devaluation of the early 1970s, India thus began the long process of reintegration with the world economy. Indeed, the 1970s saw a consistent rise in the economy's openness ratio (the share of foreign trade in GDP) [Rodrik and Subramanian 2004, Figure 5]. But a new element in international integration also emerged. The oil price hikes opened new markets in west Asia not only in terms of exports but also for Indian manpower. Remittances from Indian workers, another indicator of integration with the world economy, jumped from $ 97 million in 1972-73 to $ 470 million in 1975-76 [Joshi and Little 1994:122].

Economic stabilisation does not necessarily equate to economic liberalisation; its key purpose is to restore balance to the macroeconomy. But in this specific instance of the mid-1970s, coming as it did after a sustained bout of radicalism, and the earlier abandonment of the nationalisation of the wholesale wheat trade sent a strong signal of change in economic direction. However, this course change encompassed more than contractionary measures and covert devaluation. In a clear indication of its intent to proceed in a liberal direction, the government established a special cabinet committee in May 1975 for an export-promotion drive and went on to institute a number of measures to promote exports.

First and foremost, the government made a radical departure from its earlier hallmark of imposing restrictions on production in the name of planning and curbing monopolies. In its drive to boost non-traditional exports, the government allowed an automatic increase in production capacity of 25 per cent over five years without requiring prior permission in the case of 15 export-oriented engineering industries. More broadly, to facilitate expanded production for exports, the government shifted to automatic licensing for export-oriented industries to import raw materials and components. To the same end, it increased import entitlements for selected industries. The government also liberalised the provision of finance for the export sector at concessional rates of interest. Further, it increased the cash incentives for exports and expanded such entitlements to industries hitherto not covered, such as engineer ing, chemicals, synthetic fibres and garments. Importantly, the government took to "selective abolition of export licensing and simplification of procedure. The licensing formalities were dispensed with in regard to nearly two-thirds of the 300 items, which were subject to export licensing earlier." It was not exactly a bonfire of all controls and restrictions, but it marked a significant start for the process of liberalisation [Joshi and Little 1994:122]. One can quibble over whether this set of reforms—and equally that of the early 1980s -constitutes liberalisation or merely attitudinal change. But this much is clear—it marked a reversal of the radical course hitherto pursued. And even an attitudinal change must in a complex and continental-size economy as India's at some point translate into policy changes.

Economic liberalisation is a process. As such, it does not emerge fully evolved suddenly, all at once. Rather, it develops over a period of time and goes through several phases or stages, often marked by fits and starts. In India's case, liberalisation can be regarded as having emerged in the crucible of a crisis of enormous proportions in the economy, which then snowballed into a larger systemic crisis in the form of the declaration of the state of emergency in June 1975. Contrary to Panagariya's (2004) position, that liberalisation episode in its entirety cannot be considered as consisting of ad hoc measures; further, there was no reversal of them. The incipient or first phase of liberalisation can thus be said to have begun in the fiscal year 1974-75 or, for the sake of simplicity, roughly around 1975, and not in 1980 as some scholars have assumed. The reforms of the 1980s and 1990s can thus be regarded as second and third phases in a longer stretched-out liberalisation process. The fundamental cause in generating the first phase of liberalisation was dissatisfaction with the growth performance under the earlier economic regime over a whole decade from 1965-66 to 1974-75.

Growth under Incipient Liberalisation

Did the first phase of liberalisation starting in 1975 accelerate the growth rate in the manner that the second and third phases have done? The short answer is, yes!

Economic performance in the first few years after the change of economic course in 1974-75 is remarkably different from that during the entire previous decade. The economic growth rate in 1975-76 was 9 per cent, helped no doubt by revived agriculture following good rains, and by the discipline imposed by the state of emergency. The rates in the subsequent three years were 1.2 per cent, 7.5 per cent and 5.5 per cent. In these four years (1975-76 to 1978-79), the average growth rate was 5.8 per cent (Table 1)—the same or similar to those for the second and third phases. The growth impulses imparted by the change in economic course had thus generated a positive impact on the growth rate. Remarkably, foreign exchange surpluses also accumulated over the period.

However, the fall in the growth rate in 1979-80 or the fifth year to a negative 5.2 per cent requires explanation. Two major external shocks were the chief culprits in this particular performance: an unprecedented drought that resulted in the sharpest post-independence decline of 12.77 per cent in agricultural production and the doubling of oil prices by OPEC. The consequence of these two devastating external shocks was once again high inflation and severe deterioration in the balance of payments. A direct consequence of the external shocks, the fifth year's performance is simply an aberration, unrepresentative of the pattern of economic growth inaugurated by liberalisation's first phase.

Should 1980 Still Be Privileged as a Breakpoint?

In view of the above, it is questionable whether 1980 can be genuinely considered to constitute the break from the Hindu rate of growth, as some economists have argued. Indeed, it is precisely the recovery in the agricultural growth rate to 12.89 per cent in 1980, following the drought year of 1979 that gives the illusion of a major boost to growth in 1980-81, and thus lends plausibility to 1980 as the year marking the break. That outcome is, however, simply an artefact of the change in the forces of nature, not a consequence of any attitudinal or policy change. It seems that, persuaded by the prevailing orthodoxy of a generalised Hindu rate of growth of 3.5 per cent, these economists have arbitrarily homogenised the entire period before 1980 in relation to growth. In starting with 1980, and thus ignoring the 1975-76 to 1979-80 period, they may well have been deterred by the figure of 3.6 per cent as the average growth rate for the second-half of the 1970s, which is so uncannily close to the Hindu rate of growth. However, such a position is untenable.

The period before 1980 is not a homogeneous one, and needs to be disaggregated for an adequate analysis. One can ignore the period of the First Five-Year Plan 1951-52 to 1955-56, which did not represent any significant change in economic policy inherited from the colonial era. Following the launching of the socialism-inspired heavy industry strategy in 1956, the growth rate for the four years at the upper end of the 1950s was 3.6 per cent. It accelerated to 5 per cent in the first-half of the 1960s, but it dropped drastically thereafter, so that the average for the subsequent decade was about half, at 2.6 per cent (Table 1). In the light of this differentiated picture of pre-1980 growth, the performance of the half-decade of 1975-76 to 1979-80 has to be seen not against a mythic Hindu rate of 3.5 per cent but against the actual performance of the previous decade. Thus considered, this half decade is as much a break from the previous decade as the first half decade of the 1980s is from the assumed Hindu rate of growth.

Even when the fifth year of the second-half of the 1970s is factored into the calculation, the average for that half decade is 56.5 per cent higher than the average of 2.3 per cent for the preceding half decade. This is not very different from the 62.9 per cent increase in the growth rate for the first half decade of the 1980s (5.7 per cent) over the Hindu growth rate. Treating 1980 as marking the end of the Hindu rate of growth is therefore an artefact of the unwarranted homogenisation of the entire history of economic growth prior to 1980, and is misleading as to claims about economic liberalisation. It is 1975, and not 1980, which truly marks the end of the Hindu rate of growth as much as it does the beginning of economic liberalisation in India. This position is confirmed not only by the data provided here on growth rates but also by the data on real gross fixed capital formation [Joshi and Little 1994, Tables 5-16].

Interestingly, in employing "recent developments in time-series econometrics" to the issue precisely of structural breaks in the economy, Jessica Wallack (2003) found 1974 and 1980 to be "the two most robust break" years among four potential break dates. This finding differs somewhat from that of Rodrik and Subramanian (2004) and also from Virmani (2004); but it fits in closely with the analysis advanced here.

Why the Fixation on 1980?

If this position is correct, then it raises the question as to why the singular fixation on 1980. There are two possible explanations with a considerable degree of plausibility. One is that 1980 is a convenient benchmark, because of the initiation around that time of a larger reform and deregulation movement favouring the market over the state in some powerful countries (the UK under Thatcher and the US under Reagan), and the subsequent development of the "Washington consensus" at the international financial institutions (IFIs). Before 1980, it is assumed, there prevailed the dark age of no economic reform, while that year marked the dawn of the age of reform. Economic reform elsewhere, including India, then simply represents "policy diffusion". Interestingly, Indira Gandhi returned to power precisely in January 1980.

But such an overall impression of the reform process is misleading. If the analysis presented above is correct, then it is obvious that the policy shift to economic reform in India, coming as it did a half decade before 1980, owed nothing to emulation of a generalised reform movement abroad or to coercion by IMF. Instead, it was rooted in India's own experience with the economic performance of earlier socialist policies. Even the turn to the IMF in 1980 to cope with the external shock from OPEC's oil price hike was based on a homegrown programme rather than one imposed by the IMF [Stiles 1991, chapter 6].

The other possible explanation is that some of the influential writing on liberalisation in India has come from reformers with a background of work in the World Bank and IMF. They have also played roles of one kind or another in the liberalisation process in the 1980s and 1990s. Arvind Virmani is one example; others are Shankar Acharya, Montek Singh Ahluwalia, and Raja Chelliah. These and other reformers have justifiable pride in the part they played in India's economic reforms, though their role was largely technical in nature, and not one of policy determination. Understandably, the mental horizon of these economists may have remained focused on the post-1980 era of reforms in which the IFIs have had a significant role.

Some critics have even argued that the entry of such reformers into India's economic bureaucracy was part of a conscious design on the part of the World Bank to move the Indian state to a reformist track [Sengupta 2004]. The significant aspect, however, is that these IFI-background officials entered India's economic bureaucracy in the 1980s when economic reform had already achieved some salience. After the confusing Janata Party interregnum (1977-79), the reform process of the time, particularly in the light of Indira Gandhi's dramatic return to power in mid-January 1980, seemed like a new beginning in India's economic history. It may have seemed credibly so since Indira Gandhi inherited an economy in a shambles, with high inflation (near 20 per cent) and a looming balance of payments crisis. The year 1980 may have also seemed an appropriate watershed since India soon entered into negotiations with the IMF and, in 1981, obtained what was until then the largest loan in IMF history, undoubtedly with some reform conditionalities. Thus, it would not be unreasonable for those present at what appears to be the birth of reform to take 1980 as marking a break in India's economic policy.

But if the story narrated earlier about the first phase of liberalisation is correct, then this is a mistaken view. The shift, both in terms of economic policy and accelerated growth began in 1975, and not in 1980. While the confusion in Janata Party's economic policy is deserving of notice, it is significant that two important committees set up by its government advocated further liberalisation—the P C Alexander committee and the D R Dagli Committee. The early 1980s thus represented continuity with the policies of 1974-75 and after, not a break with them. That continuity derived from the success of those earlier policies. It is difficult therefore to agree with the proposition that Indira Gandhi changed economic course in 1980 because she had been "chastened" by her absence from power. The change had occurred earlier in 1974-75, motivated by considerations precisely of improving economic performance, not mere power.

When Indira Gandhi returned to power in 1980, she had already shed her socialist colleagues and her socialist ideology, though she continued to employ socialist rhetoric to mask her liberalisation policy. One of the first noteworthy economic policy actions of her government was the issuance of the Industrial Policy Statement in July 1980 in order to adjust the Industrial Policy Resolution of 1956 to new circumstances. Continuing the economic liberalisation inaugurated in the midst of the economic crisis in 1974-75, the new policy extended the permission for automatic expansion of capacity by 25 per cent over five years to a much larger number of industries.4 It further adopted a more liberal stance toward the import by industry of raw materials, spare parts and, especially, technology. Significantly, the number of foreign collaborations approved annually suddenly more than doubled. These various reforms were consolidated in the Sixth Five-Year Plan.5 Interestingly, when India went in for the IMF loan in 1980, it pre-empted the application of conditionalties to it on the plea of having already accomplished the necessary reforms on its own [Stiles 1991:114-15, 121, 122].

A more dramatic shift in industrial policy took place in 1982, which incorporated two new measures. One extended the principle of automatic expansion of licensed industrial capacity so as to permit expansion by one-third, rather than just one-fourth as before. The other enlarged the list of "core" industries that would be open to large industrial houses and foreign companies. Again, the government allowed the private sector to enter new areas of industrial activity, such as power and oil exploration, that were earlier closed to it.7 Further, the government abolished administered prices for pig iron and brought about the partial decontrol of cement.8 Significantly, Indira Gandhi appointed two important committees whose recommendations would have a considerable impact on subsequent policies on licensing controls and trade liberalisation.

In the light of the foregoing evidence, it is patent that all this was no "liberalisation by stealth". The new policies were part of the record, inside and outside Parliament, and were the object of public criticism and attack. It is equally obvious that the shift to favouring economic liberalisation, having taken place over the period from 1974 to 1980, had occurred prior to the government's recruitment of IFI-background economists. Consequently, the induction of such economists into India's economic bureaucracy was not the cause of the shift of opinion in the government in favour of liberalisation but the consequence of it.

The shift in intellectual opinion in favour of liberalisation at the top, that seems evident with Indira Gandhi's return to power in 1980 underlines another aspect of the reform process. Panagariya had pointed out that the success of the reforms of the 1980s had been played out, by building confidence among the politicians, which played a foundational role in the subsequent reforms in 1991. But what would then explain this risk-taking by the pushing of economic reforms in the 1980s? It would seem that it is precisely the experience of success with the reforms of 1974-75, which had been worked out in the context of a desperate economic crisis, that lay at the base of the expansionary, rather than contractionary, adjustment to the economic crisis of the early 1980s.

Conclusions

At the broader theoretical level, this case study of India's experience with economic liberalisation testifies to the robustness of the proposition of reform advocates that liberalisation makes for acceleration in the rate of economic growth. This is certainly true of the phase of liberalisation marked by the paradigm shift in economic policy in 1991. But it is equally true, as more recent work by economists has shown, of the within-system economic policy reforms of the 1980s.

More distinctively, the present case study has demonstrated that economic liberalisation should be more accurately seen as beginning in 1974-75 (rather than in 1991 or 1980), when the government headed by Indira Gandhi changed economic course. That government did so under the compulsions of an enormous economic crisis arising out of external shocks and the failure of earlier ideology-inspired economic policies. Sufficient and compelling evidence has been provided on this point. It is therefore difficult to agree with the proposition that only in 1980 Indira Gandhi "realigned herself politically with the organised private sector and dropped her previous rhetoric" about "socialism and pro-poor policies" [Rodrik and

Subramanian 2004:4]. In reality, as argued here, the change began much earlier—in 1974-75. Indira Gandhi's last phase at the head of the government from 1980 to 1984 marks no new departure, but truly represents continuity in economic policy with the reforms of 1974-75. Interestingly, in dividing India's planning experience into various phases, the eminent economist, P.N. Dhar, who was Indira Gandhi' s principal advisor and chief of staff during the 1970s, treats the third phase "1973-74 to 1984-85" as all of a piece as regards economic policy [Dhar 2003, chapter 1].

As a consequence, the issue of the credibility of reforms of the 1980s has to be seen in a different light. Virmani had attributed the patent success of the period's rather modest reforms, in considerable part, to their sharper credibility because Indira Gandhi had learnt her lesson from the consequences of her previous mistakes. If she "learnt from her own experience" indeed, she did so in 1974-75, and the credibility of her later reforms derived from her actions at that earlier time, and the successful experience of economic actors with those actions. Similarly, the success of the liberalisation policies undertaken in 1974-75 enables us to understand why Indira Gandhi continued with similar policies on returning to power in 1980. Verily, it is 1975, and not 1980, that constitutes a break in both economic policy and economic growth.

8

Liberalising Capital Account

India's experiment with reforms is poised at a crucial juncture with a clear nod from the finance ministry in favour of capital account convertibility. What does it really have in store for us? What are the experiences of the other developing countries? What is our experience with the management of the exchange rate so far? How does the Reserve Bank of India actually intervene in the market? What are the constraints faced by the apex institution? These are the questions, which usually confront a serious and diverse group of readers such as students, researchers, and policy-makers. Renu Kohli's timely book on these issues serves a great purpose by providing detailed and lucid analyses of various facets of the problem. Taking capital in and out of India without any constraint, be it for consumption or investment is essentially what is meant by full capital account convertibility. Enhancing the ability of private capital to fly out at will, often poses serious problems. Substantial capital flight may lead to severe exchange rate adjustments, interest rate upswings and closure of business units, unemployment and eventually social unrest. On the other hand, a flexible option provided to the foreign investors favourably alters the perception of the international capital market, reducing the chances of capital getting stuck in barriers. Decline in risk premiums attracts more investment, spurting growth arid providing the necessary funds for capital-starved enterprises; A more post-modern perspective will be to take into account the possibility that if an Indian investor wishes to acquire foreign business units for strategic and synergic reasons, a relatively open capital account becomes particularly useful. The problem is not one of understanding the pros and cons of such a policy but to assess its possible impact in our specific context.

If one could formally write down a kind of "social objective function" involving the costs and benefits of capital account liberalisation, the problem would boil down to weighing the "derivative" of policy initiatives, keeping in mind that the marginal cost of such a move has to receive a far greater weight than the marginal benefit. If a 1 per cent potential increase in the growth rate has to be weighed against the potential risk of unemployment and closure of numerous enterprises, a democratic nation should think deep before embarking on such a path. Therefore, one has to know about the basic theory and historical outcomes of the capital account liberalisation process.

Overview

Chapter 1 of Kohli's book starts with an overview of the problem, discussing various theoretical works and empirical evidence in a global context. Unrestricted capital flows destroy the capacity of the monetary authorities to alter interest rates and control exchange rate movements. This is undesirable from the point of view of a regulator. The main contribution of this chapter, apart from being a nice survey of the existing literature, is a fine discussion of the major competing arguments. In particular Dani Rodrik's scepticisms regarding the positive impact of capital inflows on percapita GDP growth is pointed against Sebastian Edwards' analysis of capital account openness and faster productivity growth. The general morale of the story seems to be a cautious approach, first, through the hierarchical sequencing of trade reforms and capital account reforms and then through a gradualist approach towards full capital account convertibility.

Chapter 2 deals with the operational aspects of capital account liberalisation in terms of a macroeconomic perspective. The conclusion that India's fiscal and financial reforms have not evolved fast enough is analysed in greater detail in subsequent chapters. The credibility of external sector reforms is reflected in a low rate of inflation, levels of short-term external debt, a small and reasonably sustainable current account deficit and sizable foreign exchange reserves. However, these cannot overshadow the fiscal profligacy of the central and state governments. Several indicators cited in the book denote the problem of public debt almost to the tune of a possible debt trap for the nation as a whole.

Subsequent chapters focus on the macro-economic impact of capital inflows, in particular on real exchange rate appreciation, reserves accumulation and stock market volatility. Although the book typically uses data up to 2000-01, such issues continue to occupy the centre stage of India's macroeconomic policy. A related theme evolves around the central bank's policy of sterilisation in the face of sizable accumulation of foreign exchange reserves and in apprehension of an undesired impact on money supply. The rapid pace of monetary growth is already taking a toll on debt management as a huge amount of government bonds are needed for such an operation. In the event of full convertibility of capital account, such a problem may become even more difficult to handle. This is not explicitly stated in the book. But one could draw such a conclusion from the arguments developed here.

I have found the chapter on the pace and sequencing of reform very useful from a historical perspective. It actually traces the entire history and design of specific policies, which have been pursued with eventual capital account convertibility as the target. If one needs to go back and analyse in detail how the banking sector, financial sector and external sector reforms were interrelated in the initial phase of liberalisation, this naturally becomes a very useful source to look at.

A dramatic rise in foreign capital inflow has its likely impact on the exchange rate. Greater integration with the financial market in the rest of the world leads to a more volatile response in nominal and real exchange rates. We have been experiencing an era of managed float as the RBI intervenes periodically in the foreign exchange market. The author identifies some features of exchange rate behaviour, which differ quite a bit from reform related experiences in other countries. They are—very low exchange rate volatility, thanks to the interventionist strategy of RBI, a clear break in the long-term depreciating trend of the real exchange rate and rise in foreign exchange reserves volatility, although I feel that in the last few years, such volatility must have come down. The fear of a steady and sharply appreciating rupee as a deterrent of exports has induced authorities to intervene in the market, although there is not strong evidence that a depreciating rupee is the crucial factor promoting our exports.

Problem of Plenty

In a way the possible criticism of the approach of the book will be a lack of precise theoretical foundations behind such policy-making in India. For example, one fails to find a systematic discussion on how the exchange rate is supposed to behave in the event of a liberalised capital account transaction. Usually as a developing country, hitherto insulated from international capital flows, liberalises its capital account, there is a fear that there will be severe capital flight or exchange rate fluctuations will increase substantially as capital quickly moves in and out of the country. While textbook type theoretical work suffers from too much emphasis on capital outflows. India provides a good example where managing huge capital inflows has become a real problem. Possible exchange rate appreciation and its adverse effect on our exports, sharp rise in foreign exchange reserves and its impact on monetary growth and inflation, cheaper loans abroad affecting the business of local banks, etc, all point towards a problem of dealing with "plenty". This should have come out more clearly in the analysis.

A natural cause of worry seems to be associated with the sterilisation process itself. This is nicely portrayed in the analysis of "quasi-fiscal" costs of maintaining huge resources, when interest rate on foreign assets is lower than the available domestic counterpart. Sterilisation refers to the sale of government bonds to mop up excess money supply from the system. Continuous sterilisation has led to a drastically reduced supply of stocks of tradable securities. While the author rightly points out the substantial costs of maintaining reserves, one does not find much discussion on what should determine some sort of an "optimal" reserves base. Is there any way of utilising such reserves in more productive ways? These problems do not find any ready answer in the theoretical literature. More analytical discussion on these issues would have been welcome.

Discussion on the banking sector reform is quite comprehensive and adequate. One problem, that became quite transparent during the Asian crisis, had to do with the increasing exposure of banks to foreign liabilities of short-term maturities. Any speculative flight of capital under such circumstances exposes the entire banking system and hence small depositors to serious problems. Thanks to judicious regulatory behaviour of the apex bank and the ministry of finance, Indian banks so far have not experienced a huge surge of deposits of this kind. Restrictions on bank privatisation, accumulation of foreign deposits, etc, have insulated our banks a bit from foreign disturbances. However, the scarcity of bank deposits has not been a cause of concern over the years given the general household attitude towards savings. Unfortunately strict prudential norms and moderate growth in the demand for bank credit among so-called non-risk borrowers have led banks to pile up government securities well beyond the statutory liquidity ratio requirements. Again, I felt that the book needed a chapter on what one should have expected in terms of standard theory and how the Indian case actually differed from conventional wisdom.

This brings us to the core issue of investment and growth and its relation to liberalised capital flows. One way to motivate the case for the free flow of capital is to speak of its possible positive impact on overall rate of investment, productivity and growth. The argument can be developed in two stages. First, through clarifying how sensitive foreign investment, direct or portfolio, is to the removal of restrictions and secondly, demonstrating how such investments can uplift the overall rate of investment and productivity in the economy. Since India has already experienced a gradual loosening of capital controls, some evidence is available for useful assessment.

It goes without saying that the booming stock market in India is primarily fuelled by foreign institutional investors. In fact, the Sensex belies all expectations and continues to overachieve at a formidable rate. Therefore, a complete withdrawal of restrictions on capital movement cannot be justified on the ground that the share market needs it, unless one can show that there is scarcity of funds for investment. This takes us to the second stage of analysis.

Stagnant Investment

Remarkably in the post-reform period, the overall rate of investment as a proportion of GDP has been quite stagnant. As private investment picked up a bit, public investment came crashing down. It has been pointed out elsewhere that a booming stock market and gradual decline in interest cost of borrowing could not elevate the aggregate rate of investment substantially in many countries. The current high rate of GDP growth in India again is not caused so much by an increase in the rate of physical investment, but possibly by an increase in the productivtty of capital stock. Also one is not sure whether further liberalisation in capital flows is essential for growth since no study has actually looked at that effect. Investment in infrastructure does require a facelift and there is no guarantee that such flows will solve this problem. It is quite possible that the limited amount of FDI and runaway stock markets may not have affected productivity in general, although this is the crucial factor behind our high rate of GDP growth. The tremendous performance of our share market has never been a good predictor of movements in corporate and private investment, which have increased moderately.

A more profound problem is to assess whether increasing capital flows actually affects numerous other indicators of India's development. Since we cannot afford only to dance at the growth rate, being a nation of substantially uneducated, malnourished, poverty-stricken masses, one has to judge how we can use international capital flows to solve some of our deeper problems. This is glaringly missing in the entire policy agenda and somewhat neglected in the present work. In fact, the entire macroeconomics literature on capital account convertibility or capital account liberalisation seldom raises concern over the impact of capital inflow on overall economic development. While the primary purpose of opening up capital account transactions is not to affect the health, education, and other social sectors directly, there are ways means by which foreign resources can be directed towards providing better social infrastructure. For example, with roaring foreign capital inflow, a small tax on such transactions may ease out volatility and generate public resources at the same time.

One would have appreciated a discussion on the theme of partial versus full capital account convertibility from a more analytical point of view. One aspect of such analysis would be to focus on the concern for management of such flows along with its impact on the financial sector. This is well performed by the volume, but possibly a more crucial aspect would be to judge what such convertibility has achieved so far in terms of its impact on investment, growth, productivity and employment. A clear cut econometric exercise should look at the usefulness of such a move in the Indian context. How exactly should one respond to the political urge for free capital flows when public Capital expenditure itself drops from 3.6 per cent (2004-2005) to 1.9 per cent (2005 -2006) of GDP? The success and failure of larger capital inflows in a wider socio-economic context depends a lot on complementary public investment. Such issues cannot be neglected while evaluating the performance of an apparently market-friendly policy.

All said and done, Renu Kohli's work is a very useful addition to the debate on capital account convertibility. If anyone has to be aware of the background of the debate, the theoretical and empirical evidence available so far and how exactly our monetary authorities deal with such problems, this is an ideal source material.

Rules for Fair Trade

In the market system there is a manner of equality that has both positive and negative effects. As compared to feudal or casteist systems that prescribe who can consume what, the market does not recognise the individual behind the buyer. This is a positive advance due to the market system. At the same time, the market is blind to the strengths and weaknesses and the capabilities that the buyer and seller bring to the market. Equality of access is taken to be equality of opportunity. The perniciousness of this doctrine of equality of access is seen vividly in the case of international trade. Does equal access mean equal opportunity? In the current version of the three worlds (developed, developing and least developed countries (LDCs)) equal access to each other's markets, in the absence of equal capabilities, is likely to lead to highly unequal outcomes in terms of both market shares and incomes.

Take the case of garment exports. In the MFA quota regime, countries like Bangladesh and Cambodia were able to utilise the quotas to develop some segments of garment manufacturing. It is highly unlikely that they would have been able to make this advance in the absence of exportquotas, which both set limits to exports from countries with scale advantage, like China, and enabled LDCs to pick up some market share. This is an example of infant-industry protection, not through tariffs but through quotas, and not for imports but for exports.

There have been many systems of differential access. In the colonial period, colonies had preferential access to empire markets. The now defunct MFA was the best such example of differential access. More recently the EU's Everything "But Arms (EBA) and USA's African Growth and Opportunity Act (AGOA), give some limited preferential access to a number of African countries, though often with rule of origin restrictions that serve as a method of protection. How can one generalise a system of differential access? This is the key problem that Stiglitz and Charlton deal with and they come up with a solution that is not only elegant in its simplicity, but also workable.

Discussions on differential access have usually focused on developed country markets. Among those for whom this access is sought, a distinction might be made, and nowadays is commonly made, of LDCs within the broader group of developing countries. Stiglitz and Charlton go beyond that to raise the issue of access even in regard to some developing country markets so as to promote south-south trade. The problem not only lies with developed countries with better developed technological capabilities, but also with large economies like India and China, which are able to achieve significant economies of scale. Both technological advantage and economies of scale can allow some producers to sell more cheaply than others from less developed or smaller economies. What the authors propose is: "...all WTO members commit themselves to providing free access in all goods to all developing countries poorer and smaller than themselves" (p 94). This rule would apply to all countries, developed and developing alike. Consequently, all developing countries "could expect free access to all markets with (1) a larger GDP, and (2) a larger GDP per capita" (p. 94).

The second clause would provide all developing countries access to all developed country markets. While the first clause would provide smaller and poorer countries, including but not limited to LDCs, access to large developing country markets, like China and India. While India seeks full access to developed country markets, it does not want to provide the same to poorer and smaller countries, like Bangladesh. It is interesting to note that in trade between India and Bangladesh there are specific restrictions to counter likely Bangladeshi garment exports to India. The Stiglitz-Charlton proposal would both give India access to developed country markets, and, in addition, give Bangladesh free access, without tariff or quota restrictions, to the Indian market.

Advantages

In elaborating this proposal the authors claim a number of advantages for it. (1) It involves significant liberalisation. (2) In particular, it involves significant south-south liberalisation. (3) Obligations are distributed progressively, with more obligations on developed countries, less on large developing countries, and so on. (4) Countries can manage major import threats. One should add though, not all import threats, as those for instance, now facing large sub-sectors of manufacturing in the developed economies, but import threats from economies with "cost advantages derived either from the scale of their economies (read, China and India) or technological advantages (read, developed countries)". (5) It is consistent with MFN liberalisation schemes. (6) It transforms discretionary schemes into well-defined obligations within the WTO. Rather than the current patchwork of discretionary schemes, often arrived at with great political cost, there would be clear rules and obligations. (7) The scheme includes an inbuilt flexibility that removes the need for renegotiation over time. "As countries develop and overtake others, they will, after an implementation period, lose some preferences and accept obligations to poorer countries. Alternatively, the scheme could be designed to include a 'one-way' provision so that free trade would increase monotonically in a dynamic world where rankings change" (p. 102).

Benefiting from trade, however, is not only a matter of gaining access. Access is essential; it is necessary but not sufficient. A country must also have the capacity to utilise that access. This is particularly important, given that a large part of such international trade may be in commodities where the developing country or LDC does not have already existing capacity. Comparative advantage points to the direction in which a country can develop exports. Comparative advantage, however, does not mean that a country automatically has such an export capacity. Developing the necessary knowledge, labour and management skills to manage the necessary production and supply system is something that requires adequate development policies within the country concerned. Further, development policies vary with the level of development. Here too, a "one size fits all" policy would be manifestly unjust in not allowing countries to follow policies suited to their level of development.

Stiglitz and Charlton also discuss the necessity of making trade rules that allow more room for required national policy initiatives. The Special and Differential Treatment (SDT) provisions give developing countries more latitude in the use of subsidies and more latitude in tariff reduction. While LDCs are allowed to use subsidies, the Trade-Related Investment Measures (TRIMs) agreement prohibits the use of investment performance measures, like local content and sourcing requirements, that have an effect on trade (p. 103).

Trade-Related Aspects of Intellectual Property Rights (TRIPS) is even worse in its protection of what are basically developed country technology monopolies. More than the royalty payments required, it restricts reverse engineering, which, in manufacturing history, has been an important mechanism for developing countries to catch up with developed countries. This catching up requires both access to the larger markets provided by trade with developed countries or larger economies, like China and India. It also requires freer flow of technology and knowledge, something that TRIPS restricts. Discussions of the benefits of trade usually confine attention to the benefits from comparative cost. But, access to larger markets can be a stimulus to learning, a stimulus which, as Pasinetti (1993) points out, may be more relevant in considering the benefits of international trade.

Question about Fairness

Coming back to the main point of the book under review, in what manner does the Stiglitz-Charlton proposal represent "fair" trade for all? The authors use Rawls' principle of difference that, "Social and economic equalities are to be arranged so that they are.. .to the greatest benefit of the least advantaged" (quoted in Stiglitz and Charlton, p 81). Provided that trade is of benefit, which is not always the case with LDCs as pointed out in UNCTAD (2004), then the Stiglitz-Charlton proposal does constitute an improvement in trade rules, such that the poorest benefit the most. In this sense it constitutes a Rawls improvement. If such an improvement were taken to be what constitutes fairness, then the proposal is fair. That a proposal leads to an improvement for the least advantaged can be ground for preferring this over other proposals that do not lead to such an improvement. But why is this considered fair?

Or, can there be other senses in which fairness may be understood? The imple^ mentation of the Stiglitz-Charlton proposal does not necessarily lead to the achievement of decent work for the export producers. Producers from developing countries may be integrated into buyer-driven supply chains in such a manner that the income benefit is very little, or even none at all. Or, producers in one country may be undercut by producers from another country willing to accept a lower standard of living. The proponents of the various "fair trade" movements might hold that for trade to be fair, prices paid to the producer must meet certain norms of standards of living, in community management or benefits,-and so on. That commodities produced with child labour are not fair trade is now quite generally accepted. In other words, some minimum labour standards, even if it be only that of not involving child labour, are accepted as necessary for fair trade.

There can be yet anpther meaning to fair trade. Trade clearly involves the exchange of unequal amounts of labour—a quantity of labour from developing countries, operating with lower technological levels, exchanges for a smaller quantity of labour from developed countries with higher technological levels [Pasinetti 1993]. Does this constitute unfair trade? One might well argue it to be so.

But there can be no doubt that the Stiglitz-Charlton proposal needs to be taken seriously and would institute a system of rules of access to international markets, which would benefit more the least advantaged. It is certainly superior to the equal access rules that are sought to be implemented under the WTO or the patchwork of schemes under various bilateral and regional trade agreements.

Conclusion

The theoretical analysis and empirical evidence briefly summarised here suggests that it is unwise to embark on further capital account liberalisation for India.

This conclusion is further strengthened when one examines India's experience with limited capital account liberalisation in recent years. First, liberalisation led to a large increase in FII, which has proved to be somewhat volatile. Most of the evidence suggests that capital inflows have driven stock prices and real estate prices, but stock prices have had little effect on real investment and growth [Rakshit 2006; Rao and Dutt 2006:150-51]. Second, the limited nature of liberalisation allowed India (as well as China) to escape from the Asian I financial crisis of 1997 relatively unscathed.

Third, India and China, both with capital controls, are among the fastest growing economies in the world today. One is led to ask: "If it ain't broke, why fix it?"

India, of course, may miraculously avoid the boom-bust cycles and adverse consequences of capital account liberalisation through effective regulation and macro-economic policies. But suitable regulation is hard to pursue, as shown, for instance, by the facts that: even rich countries (which liberalised their capital accounts at a far later stage of their development than India is at now) are not free from financial instability; countries as developed as South Korea had a severe currency crisis; and several financial instruments—including derivatives -are very difficult to monitor. India would not need just one miracle, but many, to ride the boom-bust waves successfully. Finally, it must not be forgotten that costs of failure are very high indeed. Per capita income in India is low and the incidence of poverty is high compared to most Latin American and east Asian countries that have suffered the consequences of the instability of capital flows: India has very little slack with which to gamble.

Bibliography

Bhagwati, Jagdish (2004): *In Defense of Globalisation,* Oxford University Press, Oxford.

Broner, F A and R Rigobon (2004): Why Are Capital Flows So Much More Volatile in Emerging Markets than in Developed Countries'! University of Pompeii.

Caballero, R. (2000):'Macroeconomic Volatility in Latin America: A View and Three Case Studies', National Bureau of Economic Research Working Paper No 77782.

Calvo, G.A., L. Leiderman and C.M. Reinhart (1996):'Inflows of Capital to Developing Countries in the 1990s', *Journal of Economic Perspectives,* Vol. 10, No 2.

Campbell, J.M. (1883): *Bombay Gazeteer;* Canara, 25(1), Central Government Press, Bombay.

Cardero, E (1984): Patron Monelario y Acumu-lacioii en Mexico, Siglo XXI-UNAM, Mexico.

Correa, E. and E Maya (2002):'Expansion de la banca extranjera en Mexico' in E Correa and A Girbn (eds). *Crisis y Futuro de la Banca en Mexico,* UNAM-M A Porrtia, Mexico.

Demir, Firat (2005): Three Essays on Financial Liberalisation, Country Risk and Low Growth Traps in Argentina,

Mexico and Turkey, unpublished Ph.D. dissertation, *Economics,* University of Notre Dame.

Dhar, P.N. (2003): *The Evolution of Economic Policy in India,* Oxford University Press, New Delhi.

Eaton, P. (19850:'Customary Land Tenure and Conservation in Papua New Guinea' in J.A. McNeely and D. Pitt (eds.), *Culture and Conservation: The Human Dimension in Environmental Planning,* Croom Helm, Dublin.

Eatwell, J. and L. Taylor (2000): *Global Finance at Risk,* The New Press, New York.

Edwards, S. (1999):'How Effective Are Capital Controls?', National Bureau of Economic Research Working Paper No 7413.

Eerumen, M.E. (2004):'La banca en Mexico'. ObservaloriodelaEi'onomiaLatinoamericana, (Internet multimedia economicjournul) March.

Frankel, J.A. (1999):'No Single Currency Regime Is Right for All Countries or At All Times', National Bureau of Economic Research Working Paper No. 7338.

Gadgil, M. and F. Berkes (1991):'Traditional Resource Management Systems', *Resource Management and Optimisation,* 18(3-4), 127-41.

Garrido, C. (2005): Desarrollo Economico y Procesos de Financiamiento en Mexico: Transformations ContemporaneasyDilemas Actuates, UAM-Siglo XXI, Mexico.

Gertler, Mark and Kenneth Rogoff (1990):'North-South Lending and Endogenous Domestic Capital Market Inefficiences', *Journal of Monetary Economics,* 26(2), October, pp. 245-66.

Griffith-Jones, S., J. Williamson and R. Gottschalk (2005): Should Capital Controls Have a Place in the Future International Monetary System, Institute of Development Studies.

Griffith-Jones, Stephany (forthcoming):'Private Capital Flows and Development: Can Boom-bust be Curtailed?' in A

Dutt and J. Ros (eds.), *International Handbook of Development Economics,* Edward Elgar, Cheltenham, UK.

Guha-Khasnobis, Basudeb and Faisal, Bari (2003):'Sources of Growth in South Asian Countries', in Ahluwalia and Williamson (eds), *The South Asian Experience with Growth,* Oxford University Press, New Delhi. India.

Guha-Khasnobis, Basudeb, and Sugata Marjit (2005),'Financial Reforms, Investment and Growth: Analytical Issues Related to the Developing Countries', Conference Paper. United Nations University, WIDER. July 1-2.

Guilien, A. (2000): Mexico Hacia el Siglo XXI: Crisis y Modelo Alternativo, UAM-Plaza y Valdes, Mexico.

Henry, Peter (2000a):'Stock Market Liberalisation. Economic Reform, and Emerging Market Equity Prices', *Journal of Finance,* 50 (2), pp 529-

Jha, Prem Shankar (1980): *India: A Political Economy of Stagnation,* Oxford University Press, New Delhi, p 171.

Joshi, Vijay and IMD Little (1994): *India: Macroeconomics and Political Economy, 1964-1991,* World Bank, Washington, DC.

Kaminsky, G. and C. Reinhart (1999): The Two Crises: The Causes of Banking and Balam of Payments Problems', *American Econom Review,* 89, 473-507.

Kaminsky, Graciela (forthcoming):'International Capital Flows to Emerging Economies: Blessing or curse?' in A. Dutt and J. Ros (eds), *International Handbookof Development Economics,* Edward Elgar, Cheltenham, UK.

Kaminsky, Graciela and Carmen Reinhart (1999):'The Twin Crises: the Causes of Banking and Balance of Payments Problems', *American Economic Review,* 89(3), June, pp 473-500.

Kaminsky, G., S. Lizondo and C. Reinhart (1998):'Leading Indicators of Currency Crises', *International Monetary Fund Staff Papers,* 45, 1-48.

Keynes, John Maynard (1936): The General Theory ofEmployment, Interest and Money, Macmillan, London.

Macedo, M A (2000):'La dinamica financiera y la tendencia a la dolarizacion de las economias latinoamericanas', *Realidad Economica,* No 175, October-November.

Marjit, Sugata (2005),'Financial Sector Reform for Stimulating Investment and Economic Growth: The Indian Experience', www.adb.org/Documents/Reports/Consultant/TAR-IND 4066/macroeconomics/marjit.pdf.

Markets, Portfolio Capital Flows and Long-Term Economic Growth: Micro and Macro-economic Perspectives', *World Development,* Vol. 26, No. 4.

Minsky, Hyman (1982): Can'It' Happen Again? Armonk. M E Sharpe, New York.

Mishkin, F S (1999):'Lessons from the Asii Crisis', National Bureau of Economic Resean Working Paper No 7102.

Moreno-Brid, J C (1999):'Mexico's Economic Growth and the Balance of Payments Constraint: A Cointegration Analysis', *International Review of Applied Economics,* Vol. 13, No. 2, May.

Moreno-Brid, J C. P Ruiz and J C Rivas (2005):'NAFTA and the Mexican Economy: A Look Back on a Ten-Year Relationship', *North Carolina Journal of International Law and Commercial Regulation,* Vol. 30, No. 4.

Nayar, Baldev Raj (1989): *India's Mixed Economy: The Role of Ideology and Interest in Its Development,* Popular Prakashan, Bombay.

Nayyar, Deepak (2002):'Capital Controls and the WorldFinancialAuthority:WhatCan We Learn from the Indian Experience?' in J. Eatwell and L. Taylor (eds). *International Capital Markets,* Oxford University Press, Oxford.

Ocampo, Jose Antonio (2003):'Developing Countries' Anti-cyclical Policies' in A. Dutt and J. Ros (eds), *Development Economics and Structuralist Macroeconomics,* Edward Elgar, Cheltenham.

Panagariya, Arvind (2004):'Growth and Reforms during 1980s